Ursu

by Sarah Napier

Sold to raise awareness and hopefully a little in the way of funds for Monica's Romanian Rescue, the charity in Romania which rescues dogs in the most difficult of circumstances, cares for them and tries to rehome them.

Without Monica Teodorescu many more dogs will die in the most horrendous and inhumane conditions than is already the case.

Thank you for buying this book.

www.monicasromanianrescue.com

JJ Moffs Independent Book Publisher Ltd
Grove House Farm, Grovewood Road, Misterton,
Nottinghamshire DN10 4EF

ISBN 978-0-9957881-0-7

Typeset and cover design by Anna Richards

FOREWORD

Born on the streets of Bucharest, Romania, Ursu was caught and flung into one of the country's most notorious kill shelters where miraculously, against all the odds, he survived several years before catching the eye of someone living thousands of miles away in the UK.

Unwanted for the first seven years of his life, broken, terrified and unapproachable, this tells the story of how a feral and badly abused dog, already approaching his senior years, gradually learned to let go of his fears and anchor his trust in humans, the very species responsible for his years of incarcerated misery.

Never give up on a dog

When we think about a feral canine we likely conjure up images of a dog that has never had contact with humans, possibly living its life out in forest or open landscape, not having experienced human interaction. But the meaning of feral is 'wild, untamed, undomesticated, untrained.' And this was Ursu, aged between seven and nine, when he joined my husband and me in January 2015. The saying 'you can't teach an old dog new tricks' is probably one of the oldest proverbial sayings around, with citations of it going back to the 16th century relating to shepherdry and the training of dogs. A saying so commonly used in today's everyday language it acted as a cautionary warning against taking a risk on an ageing dog that had never obeyed a word of human command and indeed had grown to fear people. Yet Ursu put paid to this in a way that encourages me to say 'never give up on a dog'. Get it right, and with patience and full commitment, most dogs will respond positively. Ursu is living proof.

A dog has no idea how we want it to behave. An obvious comment given we're human and a dog is a dog. But it's easy to overlook this, unconsciously relying on the innate intelligence of a dog to do the understanding. Over time they work out for themselves the real demands we are making of them through all our mixed messages and inconsistencies. But in reality it's our job as humans to assist a dog to become socialised and to do this kindly and in a consistent manner. A badly behaved dog isn't a bad dog; a terrified dog even less so.

The majority of dogs come to owners who love them, with sufficient trust in their hearts to enable the incomparable bond that exists between man and dog to develop quickly without problems. But how do you get anywhere near a dog whose only relationship with man has been non-existent at best and brutal at worst? A dog that has survived on its own wits without the back-up of pack protection and with no intention of letting a human get close? A dog that is not just feral but with a learnt distrust of humans.

This is the story of Ursu (Romanian for Bear) and his transformation from unapproachable to affectionate, obedient (mostly!) and happy. Simply put, with patience and consistency, and trying all the while to think like a dog and not like a human it is never too late to turn a dog around, even a senior one. Ursu's acquired behaviour was the direct result of human aggression, not an inherent bad streak. But at middle-age his behaviour had become so embedded that whilst the principles of dog behaviour may be easy to grasp, the reality of trying to get an erstwhile terrified dog to trust was a long haul.

Why a dog from Romania?

I've loved dogs since I was a small child and over the years have come to favour helping rescue dogs. Our last wonderful pet Daisy, a Golden Retriever, came to live with us aged six and left us just before her 17th birthday. As a rescue dog she arrived with some nervous traits but these soon ironed themselves out and she went on to become a grand dog unfazed by anybody or anything. Daisy was your typically laid-back retriever happy to do what dogs do without labouring herself with bigger thoughts. So amiable was she that she continued on, living happily with us through loss of sight and hearing, enjoying her food, walks and socialising, and we only took the heart-rending decision to say goodbye to her when she became miserable through lack of mobility in her back legs. We'd also had to put

4

to sleep our Labrador/Collie mix Lizzie, our dog before Daisy, at the age of nine, having gone from bullet-proof healthy to terminally ill with cancer and unable to stand within a matter of weeks. Heart-breaking as it is to take the decision, we're so lucky that we can offer this timely kindness to our animals.

After Daisy left us my husband and I spent a year catching up on our freedom having spent the last twelve months of her life pretty much tied to home, which we'd been comfortable with, content to look after Daisy for as long as she wanted to be here. And then in the autumn of 2014 the feeling was building again that I wanted another dog to come live with us. My philosophy is that whilst ever I am grieving over a lost pet there is another rescue dog out there waiting for its chance. The sooner I recover, the sooner I can make another dog happy. The love goes on. I was open to breed and source, I just wanted a dog that caught my eye and that I felt a connection with. All dog lovers will know this feeling and that sometimes explaining why a particular dog gets to us is hard to rationalise.

So it was with Ursu, advertised on a well-known UK website that promotes all manner of animals both for sale and adoption. Many people have asked, sometimes quite critically, why adopt an animal from abroad when there are so many in this country needing a home. The simple answer is Ursu was the dog that pulled on my heart-strings at the time of looking. I'd made enquiries of other rescue dogs in this country too but for various reasons they didn't come to fruition. It's like asking why we do anything for anyone or anything abroad rather than within our own nation. I consistently donate to various charities, including animal charities in this country, and do some local voluntary work, but when I was looking for a dog to come live with me, hopefully for a very long time, it was

5

Ursu I felt was waiting for me. It's a free choice and we can all choose to do a bit of everything. As it happens I thought I was enquiring after a bitch - we've always had bitches in the past - but after contacting the UK volunteer about Ursu it soon became clear that she was in fact a 'he' and considerably older than first thought - probably between seven and nine - certainly no younger as his life had been tracked. What is more, the volunteers had recently taken the tough decision, based on information coming from Romania, that Ursu was beyond help and were about to take him down from the advertisement site. He had become so traumatised by his life events that it was felt he could never be homed (not re-homed, as he'd never had one). It was considered that it would be irresponsible. He wouldn't let anyone approach him and this could only be done either through 'netting' or sedation. We were the only enquiry he'd received throughout his life and at the time I made it the volunteers had just agreed that he would spend the rest of his days in a Romanian shelter.

And so with a feeling that this random timing of mine couldn't result in such a sad ending for such a dog I began to delve more into Ursu's story. His saviour had been Monica in Romania, a living saint who spends her days as a school teacher and all her spare time, with the help of her husband and daughter, saving as many animals from the kill shelters as she can for re-homing. Whilst waiting for their forever homes they live in other Romanian shelters with slightly better conditions than the one Ursu had been incarcerated in or in foster homes, sponsored by the volunteers. A few dogs with individual needs were living outside in Monica's backyard. With the head volunteer being in the UK, the majority of Romanian strays get re-homed over here in the UK but a significant number, again through the UK volunteers, transfer to other parts of

Europe, with France, Belgium and Germany also very much in the picture. Monica now has her own website set up with the help of the UK volunteers (www.monicasromanianrescue. com) and since Ursu joined us in 2015, with great fortitude and additional fund-raising, Monica has gone on to secure a piece of land and with the help of her family and friends has developed a purpose-built shelter for the animals where she can care for them as well as she can, ensuring good diets and healthcare. The volunteers work tirelessly. These dogs and cats (and even a horse) come to Monica from the public kill shelters, the streets and surrounding fields and with her building reputation many simply get dumped outside her home.

The public kill shelters are a story in themselves and can be googled for a greater insight into the appalling, barbaric conditions.

Ursu was originally in the Cornetu kill shelter in Bucharest, which, along with Mihailesti, are known to be two of the worst kill shelters in Romania. Anyone with the stomach to google Cornetu can see for themselves the dreadful state of the place. Personally I cannot even listen to the horrors of the establishment, dogs screaming with fright and from pain, let alone look at the internet visual revelations. But it's good that people stronger than me can, and that exposure of the barbaric practices handed out to the dogs get exposed for the atrocities that they are.

A stray dog enduring a Romanian winter

Ursu's life in Romania

Over time my husband and I have pieced together most of Ursu's story. As succinctly as possible without sensational embellishment (for readers will be able to picture the horror for themselves), this is the life we gradually came to learn had been Ursu's for his first seven or so years:-

Ursu survived for about two years on his own on the streets of Bucharest living off his wits and dodging the street catchers before eventually being caught and dumped in Cornetu shelter. The usual means of capture is the use of wire lassos from a moving van that tightens to almost strangulation enabling the dog catchers to sweep the dog off the ground and chuck it into the van without slowing down. Many are trussed up alive with their legs at painful angles. The catchers are paid for each dog delivered to the kill shelters whether deposited dead or alive, or badly injured. Once at Cornetu Ursu was castrated without anaesthetic.

Ursu existed without regular food and alternated between a single cell and a shared hut, airless and windowless, living amongst his and other dogs' faeces, the dying and the dead, through heat wave summers and sub-zero winters. The dogs survived on water, and scraps brought in ad-hoc by volunteers; also by eating the diseased dead carcasses which they fought over. The dogs were regularly culled through bludgeoning and poison which Ursu regularly witnessed and heard.

Ursu was in Cornetu for two to three years, all the while surrounded by disease and the dead. The understanding is he was permitted to survive because he somehow remained healthy amidst the woeful conditions and was among the few robust animals guaranteeing a sustained monthly income to the owner. These monies came via contributed EU funding designed to combat the irrefutable overrun of dogs in Romania. The then owner continually refused all monetary offers from Monica to get Ursu out. She had regularly seen him when she, along with other volunteers, would visit the shelter to throw scraps to the starving dogs. That was until the local Mayor decreed that Cornetu was housing too many dogs and that the owner was going to have to kill the healthy ones too to reduce the numbers. At that point Ursu became profitable only through bribery and at a cost of 200 Euros Monica saved Ursu and other dogs too at additional cost. Until that time the owner had hitherto only been willing to 'sell' to Monica the sick and the dying.

Ursu was unapproachable and had to be 'netted' in order to be transferred to Dog Town – a better shelter on the outskirts of Bucharest, with an exercise area where volunteers could let the dogs have snatched moments of movement, but nevertheless still a kill shelter with regular culls and lacking the basics that our UK rescue centres offer. His board and keep were funded by the UK volunteers' fundraising efforts and this extended to the commissioning of a dog behaviourist to try and help Ursu to let go of his terror and relax but they couldn't get anywhere near him in that environment. He was mostly quiet and distant but would emit a low continuous growl if anyone made a step towards him.

After a further year of his now seven to nine year life Monica's Romanian Rescue took the responsible but sad decision that Ursu was too far gone and too damaged to be helped and that he must live out his life in Dog Town. This decision was taken around the time of my enquiry and also around the same time Monica learned that there was to be another imminent cull at Ursu's new shelter. She intended getting her five or so sponsored dogs that were fielded out there back to her home backyard and safety, Ursu hopefully being one of them.

The UK volunteers couldn't have been more straightforward with me about the timing and about Ursu's unsociable behaviour. They offered up alternative dogs for me to consider, all of them badly in need of a home and some love. But it had become that situation we'll all be familiar with in some guise or another where, having once seen a plight it becomes impossible to walk past it, regardless of logic. We were told that we had been his only enquiry in all his life. My heart went out to him. The feeling was visceral. I simply couldn't accept that a dog that had managed to survive unrepeatable horrors against the odds for such a sustained length of time could be left, at best, to wither. Such a stoic dog deserved a chance. I said to myself that as dogs mentally live in the present, why would day 1,400 of the same environment be any less terrifying than day one? Maybe, I thought, he just needed to be in another world if he was to stand a chance of successful rehabilitation. These high hopes were, of course, nothing more than aspiration and conjecture. Common sense told me to be philosophical, to move on and not to assume I could be of help to him. It's not like there's a shortage of dogs looking for a family to join. My husband and anyone else who has knowledge about dogs whose opinion I sought reinforced what I knew to be true. Ursu, sad as his case was, sounded beyond hope and to somehow get him here from another country, a job in itself, on the slim chance he would settle, was unrealistic head in the clouds romance.

Added to Ursu's feral behaviour we didn't know what physical state of health he was in other than apparently looking OK. We also didn't know what mixture of breed he was. It was clear he was a Heinz 57 but maybe he had a dominant streak of some kind. We simply didn't know. My husband also, understandably, had strong misgivings about taking on another senior dog so close on the heels of Daisy, with all the constraints this places on personal freedom if an elderly dog is to be looked after compassionately. I couldn't argue with any of the objections. I agreed with them all and acknowledged it was a bad idea. Yet at the same time I felt compelled to give it a go. I was in tears at the thought of this dog, having survived so long without love and kindness, at best ending its life behind bars without so much as having been given a walk, and at worst being killed barbarically through bludgeoning in the next cull if Monica and her husband found him too difficult to catch and take home with them.

After much persuasion and over a glass of wine at the kitchen table my husband, on a handshake, agreed to support me in my wish that we take on Ursu, on the condition I took main responsibility for the dog's training. Also that Ursu 'went' if he couldn't become socialised to the point he could be trusted amongst people, and particularly children. My husband was adamant about this. If Ursu remained a dangerous dog he would have to go. I was happy. If Ursu only progressed to the point where we could get a lead on him and he sat in our English country garden tied to a long rope, experiencing the outdoors and receiving love and good food and warmth and care, it would be a far, far better life than the one he was currently experiencing. It was worth a punt.

I should say at this point that Ursu is just one Romanian story. And Romania is just one country. There are around 65,000 stray dogs in Bucharest alone. There are other heart-breaking situations of all types of cruelty, from dogs having been purposely blinded with sand, rendered part- paralysed by tethering, being turfed out onto the streets when pregnant, elderly, or needing veterinary attention. They get beaten to death, burnt alive, poisoned. Romania has violated the Convention for Animal Welfare. The story of Ursu is unusual in that he survived for so long in terrible standards of incarceration for up to four years. The majority get out sooner either through death or rehoming. How he physically survived is a mystery to everyone. But there was also the mental abuse. It had been huge and unremitting for an extended period of time and it was anyone's guess as to whether it had left a permanent mark. Under attack there are those of us who cower and those of us who react defensively. I reckoned on Ursu, who was quiet other than growling or running away if anyone approached, of being the latter. A dog that was simply demonstrating spirit and

The advertisement of Ursu that first caught my eye, taken years before our enquiry

intelligence. He was spot-on right not to trust. I felt his eyes told me that at heart he was a soft dog. I just hoped I was right.

Were we the right match?

But it wasn't just down to us and my choice as to whether I was willing to take on Ursu and give it a go. Monica's UK volunteers take their task seriously and responsibly and the other side of the coin was whether I was the right person for the dog. It's all very well having a softness for a particular animal and a cherished hope that things will be good, but the day-to-day reality is quite different. We would have a daily grind ahead of us, with this dog requiring concentrated and committed effort with uncertain outcome. Also, did I have what it takes to do this? I'm not qualified in dog psychology and whilst I've loved dogs since I was a small kid earning the trust of strays whilst I lived in Singapore as a child, this was a very different number.

We had a home visit from a UK volunteer of Monica's Romanian Rescue which we passed with an understanding that this was an unusual situation. I stressed that I was serious and my commitment was great enough that if there was a shred of light I would find it and work with it. I also didn't envisage that this would be a dog that would ever be let out of our sight outdoors, if we even progressed that far with him. It was important, knowing what we did about the dog, that we wouldn't be putting the rest of the neighbourhood in jeopardy of his unpredictable and possibly aggressive behaviour. Big gamble all round. The last thing Monica and her family needed after all her tireless and dedicated help towards these wretched souls was for me to undo all her and the volunteers' good work through the bad publicity an uncontrollable dog would attract. And just when the charity was starting to overcome prejudice and assumptions by some people that it was a money-making racket. It was wrong for me to damage the charity's hard-won reputation because of my strong personal wish.

It was put to me by the volunteers that maybe, given that Ursu would, in the interim, hopefully be living in Monica's back yard in his escape from the imminent culling, that it might be a good idea to first bring in a dog behaviourist. Then, after six months, if his reactions had improved that would be a more appropriate time for him to come to us. This sounded sensible except for the fact that Ursu was already judged to be about nine. He would be 10 by the time he had his chance of a home and might have developed health issues making it a no-goer for us so soon after Daisy, as I'd accepted my husband's argument that we wouldn't knowingly so soon walk into another situation of being 'confined to barracks'. And then what were the chances of someone else taking him? My husband and I are also just one-dog households and the option of waiting another six months dog-less on the off-chance we would be joined by Ursu seemed remote. I was also afraid that given that his six months' probation period would still be in a kennel situation living outdoors with about twenty other strays of Monica's, that progress would be insufficiently significant to prove to us all that he could be turned around. In a nutshell I worried that this sensible offer of help might ironically work counter-productively for him. So we decided to go for it and I went into it with open eyes and a strong sense of responsibility. The next question was how to get a dog from Romania to England that won't take even a collar, let alone a lead.

The charity wouldn't take any money from me until the details had been ironed out and whilst on the subject of costs the price in 2015 for getting Ursu to us was £250.00: £175.00 in overland transport costs and the balance of £75.00 contributing to vaccinations, passport and micro chipping and the multiple years of his sponsored keep.

'They've got him'

I was on absolute tenterhooks the day Monica and her husband were due to retrieve their five or so dogs from Dog Town in advance of the planned cull for that weekend. I was nervous that Ursu would be too vicious to catch, time would run out, and Monica would have to become philosophical and leave him behind. There are literally thousands of Romanian dogs in need of help and no one dog is any more important than another. But, of course, I've since come to appreciate what a determined person Monica is.

When I received this photo later the same day saying 'They've Got Him' my heart lurched. He had his body turned away, but he was interested. A good sign. I have no idea whether they netted him or sedated him – he certainly wouldn't have gone quietly. But Monica and her husband were truly brilliant that day and it can't have been easy. Not just the physical difficulty of collecting up Ursu, but also as the massive dog lovers that they are, knowing that their five were the lucky ones. Scores more would be dead just days later. That Saturday, familiar with the methods by which these dog numbers are reduced, I felt so sad. Once again Ursu had 'dodged the bullet' and I was so thankful for that - without the prospect of a home his behaviour would have meant certain death either this time around or in the future - but my overriding feeling that day was despondency. Heaven knows how Monica finds the strength to keep going.

The very day after Ursu got out of Dog Town I received a snippet of video of him in Monica's backyard. Whilst nervous and jittery he was evidently perky and coping and, for just two seconds, tolerated without an aggressive response, the touch of Monica's husband, before flinching and darting out of sight. So his legs could move and he could see. It had taken less than 24 hours after joining Monica's family for his behaviour to begin to change. "He knows we've saved him", said Monica.

Dogs are intelligent and I took heart that my first instincts about Ursu's behaviour were hopefully right. Monica was amongst those people who Ursu hadn't allowed approach him whilst in both of the kill shelters. Yet in the care of these same people in an environment where he could literally smell the mood of his fellow strays, he knew he was somewhere different. After years spent scavenging on the streets for food, avoiding traffic, fending for himself through all weathers and then being harshly caught and thrown into a living hell for years on end, he'd picked up instantly that these other dogs in Monica's care weren't in fear of their lives. All thoughts of providing him with a dog behaviourist were abandoned. What he needed was a safe haven and concentrated one-to-one love and training

Preparing for Ursu's arrival

The British astronaut, Tim Peake, remarked on his arrival back from the International Space Station in June 2016 after a six month stint in space, how strong the earth smelt. Whilst not on quite the same dramatic scale as a mission to outer space, we nevertheless imagined a similarity for Ursu. He had been in an airless hut for over two years, followed by a year in a concrete cell and without the mental references to be able to rationalise it. The year he spent in the better shelter Dog Town, sponsored by fundraisers, had given him the opportunity to stretch his legs with volunteers on a patch of land attached to the shelter, but he was too scared to let anyone touch him, opting instead to look out on his small world of concrete and fencing. He hadn't walked as such for about three years. Also, he'd heard few kind voices and certainly knew no commands. He knew his name, Ursu, given to him by the volunteers, but he wouldn't respond other than to look up at the sound of his name and to let out a low growl if anyone thought they might try and befriend him.

So, in preparation for his arrival with us, we decided to begin by creating an environment that enabled him to take in the world at his own pace without threat. We imagined everything would be new to him - noise, space, objects and people - and he wouldn't know what to make of any of it and would need time if he was to learn to let go of his anxieties. He possibly had never seen grass to speak of and he certainly had never enjoyed the indoors, electricity, vibrancy, colour, or tasty food in recent years. His life was grey, flat, sedentary, boring and monotonous, interspersed by periods of fear. He had none of the comforts we think of as the very basics we give our dogs, even those in UK shelters.

We decided to configure a shelter space for him that would mimic what he was familiar with. But rather than it be a cold damp concrete outdoor shelter, we designed one indoors offering warmth and comfort. But it shouldn't be too warm, we calculated, as Ursu had only ever survived outdoors and through winters that could hit minus 20 degrees centigrade overnight and he needed to acclimatise gradually. Many puppies lose their lives during Romanian harsh winters; even some of those gathered up by Monica and kept as warm as possible. In the weeks leading up to Ursu joining us, Romania was having a particularly cold spell of minus 22 degrees overnight and whilst he wouldn't have been actively enjoying the Romanian cold, we didn't want to stress him with too much sudden change. My husband and I share a carpeted office with full windows that overlook our quiet garden which is at the front of the house and we could moderate the heat, separate from the rest of the house. We cordoned off an area to the front of the office measuring about 11 feet square and set up a crate big enough for him to stand up and turn around in and which we put a dog blanket on top of, as well as inside, to give him a den-like feeling of security. We added a soft day bed by its side. We also had an old sofa and a couple of chairs in this space. Furniture would be novel to Ursu and we had no idea how he would respond to inanimate objects and whether they would represent a threat or something to be wrecked.

One thing we were certain of is that he wouldn't take a collar – and if he wouldn't take a collar then he certainly wouldn't take a lead. He'd clearly been traumatised by the lasso wire and this cruel style of capture is enough to kill some of the dogs. Many also have their legs then tied up behind them at an excruciating angle. We didn't know whether Ursu had also suffered this. Then there was the house-training. A dog that has spent numerous years simply defecating wherever it has stood, could it be house-trained and if so, how long would this take? We really would be working from basics and there would be no question of being able to take him to dog training. We were going to have to invest ourselves totally and just hope some general understanding and commitment would get us through.

We placed the crate immediately next to the door of the office leading out into the garden to reduce any stress he might have about being indoors for the first time in a spacious environment; also to help with toilet training hoping that what we wanted him to do became naturally obvious to him. We certainly didn't want to have to talk at him relentlessly. The human voice was scary and he would have no idea what we were asking of him anyway. Basically, by keeping his boundaries small, quiet and comfortably familiar, but with a sense of the outdoors, we were attempting to gradually alleviate his terror.

I bought a collar and lead and, given the circumstances, opted for a clip-on soft synthetic one as thin as possible whilst still substantial and a matching plain neutral-coloured lead. I wore these round my neck a few times before his arrival to give them my scent. The idea was that if he learnt to accept me, he might by association accept an object carrying my body smell. I was willing to try anything.

His name. One school of thought is that it can help rehabilitate a dog by changing its name from one it associates with abuse, to a fresh one. And so I decided upon Nelson. It struck me as being a good boy name and one appropriate to a beating heart that has spent years behind bars and emerged sane, or at least I hoped sane. In reality there was every chance he would display stress-associated behaviour. The name Nelson also meant I wouldn't have to continually be explaining his unusual name of Ursu, although my husband and I did like it.

My husband purchased some books on dog psychology as part of my 2014 Christmas stocking which I read avidly. I've also always been a keen viewer of TV programmes on animal psychology and patterns of behaviour and it was important that I soak up as many hints and tips as I could well in advance so that I could apply them naturally without too much unsuccessful experimentation.

The month before he joined us

As I've mentioned, the rescue organisation was loath to take any money from us until the last minute and with this carried the option for me to change my mind about taking on Ursu at any point. It had also been agreed that if I simply couldn't handle him that he would be taken away. Where, I didn't know and I didn't ask. I'd face that if and when I had to. If I examined the possibilities now it wouldn't serve anything. But it did bring home to me yet again that my desire to try and work with Ursu was dragging others into my self-inflicted predicament and requiring the preparation of contingency plans.

With it being close to Christmas and what would be a noisy house-full at ours, we'd asked to take Ursu in early January 2015. Ursu would spend the gap of about five weeks in Monica's outdoor shelter, the base for those most needing her full attention such as the puppies and the ill and frail. Before the erection of Monica's purpose-built shelter in 2016, the remainder of the strays were either fielded out to other shelters or in foster care, a large expense for the charity.

The reputable British transport company used by the charity had agreed to transport Ursu without the usual requirement of sporting a collar and they also promised to ensure that his journey was as stress-free as possible. The arrangements for the dogs travelling from Romania are explained on the website (www.monicasromanianrescue.com) and couldn't be more straightforward, simple and legitimate. And also swift. Ursu was with us within five days of leaving Romania.

It's because Ursu had been in the system for such an extraordinarily long time that the rescue organisation were so familiar with his story. As the weeks went by and we received follow-up news of Ursu's progress, I began to wonder whether I was doing the right thing in taking him on myself. Monica and her family had known Ursu so long that there was a certain affinity of sorts and it was, after all, Monica who had saved him and not me. When I received a photo of Monica's then nine-year old daughter in the pen of dogs with Ursu positioned close to her it became clear that this wasn't a fundamentally savage dog. Frightened, untrained, unpredictable and an unknown quantity certainly, but not a complete write-off. So why, I began to ask myself, would I traumatise an already frightened dog, and a middle-aged to senior one at that, by hauling him over to the UK with all the stresses and strains of travel involved to an unknown new world. Maybe it would be kinder to keep him in Monica's shelter, an environment, if not a cosy home, at least one he was familiar with and which he wasn't fearful of. It was enough for me that he was still alive and had a chance of kindness. I just wanted the best for him. I didn't need to own him.

I began to toy with the image of a growing bond between Ursu and his new family and that maybe my contribution would be best delivered financially to help support his keep. The response I got from Monica via the volunteers – who handle and sift all the two-way adoption process – is that if we were willing to take on Ursu, she could then go on to help another dog. In short, every dog adopted creates a space for Monica to save another. She loves them all. This made perfect sense to me. We help on a micro level. Monica saves on a macro level. Fostering of dogs in Romania is for financial reasons and Ursu wouldn't have been given the one-to-one attention he now needed if he had gone elsewhere within the country.

The big day

On Saturday 10 January 2015, a date forever etched in my mind, my husband and I travelled together down the M1 to the Midlands to one of the central pick-up points for the dogs, harbouring a mixture of both excitement and trepidation. For my husband it was mainly trepidation. Ursu and his fellow companions heading to homes up north had travelled up from Essex that morning and as the doors of the van opened Ursu was the first dog on show. He sat in his individual crate at floor level, with another dog above him, a scene replicated down the line of the van. I remember doing a thumbs-up to my husband who was still sat in the car. To me this dog looked gorgeous and I was smitten all over again. He was also calm and appeared to have a collar on. Great, I thought. This dog is OK and I began to feel less uneasy. Alas I'd allowed myself to be lulled into a false sense of confidence. The picture quickly changed. The driver opted to get Ursu off and out first. I was beginning to sense he'd been a bit of a handful.

It's a requirement when collecting a dog to take along personal identification and also a slip lead so that the dog can be quickly contained as it comes out of its crate, enabling easy transfer to the new owner, complete with the passport and vaccination paperwork. The paperwork side of things went without a hitch but the moment the crate was opened and Ursu saw the slip lead he did the 'Wall of Death' as my vet has since come to call it. Sheer and utter terror kicked in. Screaming and bucking and throwing his body this way and that, Ursu was uncontrollable. And also strong. One witness said that in his fright he soiled himself but in the pandemonium I don't recall it. I have since learned that many of the dogs in the kill shelters defecate through sheer fear at the mere sight of approaching staff.

I have no memory of how I got the slip lead on but it was with the driver's assistance who was shouting that Ursu would bite through it within seconds and we needed to act. If he had have done he would have been up the M1 within minutes. The driver took over the situation and somehow managed to grab Ursu and hold him in a position preventing his escape, all the while with Ursu continuing to writhe and scream and snap. With further team effort – I imagined there'd been a lot of team effort to get him this far and pass the requisite health checks in Essex - the driver carried Ursu over to our car all the while keeping a tight hold on him and Ursu withstood it, maybe sensing there was no escape. All three of us nudged Ursu into the crate positioned in the back of our car and closed the gate across. It was like the flick of a light switch. In the space of a second he returned to calm. The transformation was startling but I was a little shaken. Pictures of metal lassos came to my mind and the clear knowledge that this dog's awful life experiences had become part of his DNA.

Driving back up the M1 to Yorkshire Ursu remained chilled, taking a quiet interest in his surroundings. He was a little jet-lagged looking, scruffy and rather smelly, but then what dog wouldn't that hadn't been groomed its entire life. As we parked up in our drive he stood up in his crate and started to excitedly wag his tail and I thought maybe the worst was over. Optimism was something I needed to hang on to. I was wrong. My husband had built a barricaded area for him over by our garage and having let him out of his crate directly into the constructed area of earth and grass - whereupon he immediately did his toilet - he then once again spiralled into a blind panic within a fraction of a second. I believe, linking back to Tim Peake's observations about the smell of earth, that he went into sensory overload and not knowing where he was and in an unprotected open space, a mist came down over his brain. To this day we don't understand how he did it but he somehow managed to squeeze his rounded Collie size frame through a gap of less than six inches and started racing back and forth across the lawn. Having already done a stunt that would have impressed Houdini and not knowing whether he could jump walls there was every chance he would soon be off, and just run and run and run. He was micro chipped but it would be Monday before I could change ownership to me and in the meantime we had no idea what would happen. Our house abuts fields with a zero tolerance of loose dogs by the farmer and at the end of our long drive was the main road through the village. We had no alternative but to start chasing him, well aware that this would be associated with his dog catching experiences in Romania and simply add to his state of blind panic. Somehow, more through luck than design, my husband managed to corner him at the far end of our garden about 120 feet away, between our summer house and the dividing stone wall between us and the farmer's field. Anticipating he might scale this three foot wall my husband lurched towards him grabbing him by his front legs and back haunches and began the huge effort of trying to keep this writhing, biting dog down. Only because it was a cold January day was my husband wearing gloves otherwise it would have been his bare hands and not the gloves that took the brunt of Ursu's teeth.

Catching up with them seconds later I felt shame at having been such a romantic idiot and entertaining, even for a second, the notion that love and patience would turn this dog around. I'd been naïve and stupid and had dragged a lot of other people into my nonsense. Ursu's bared teeth – those still remaining - were discoloured, the back ones dark brown, almost black. What had I done?

And then something happened. After what seemed an age but was probably about two minutes, Ursu went limp. My husband hadn't made any attempt to hurt him in those 120 seconds, rather he was just firmly not risking releasing his grip, keeping Ursu captive on the ground keeping a tight hold on both front and back legs. And so the dog chose to surrender. It was a frightening start but a defining moment that we think fast-forwarded this dog's rehabilitation. My husband had had every opportunity to hurt this dog – that's what Ursu had come to expect – yet it hadn't happened.   Not even a booted kick. Ursu had only been in our care for three hours and it had almost ended in disaster.   And I couldn't forgive myself for that. It could just have easily have gone the other way. We would never have seen Ursu again – that was for sure.   But luck was on our side.   Ursu had unwittingly run towards an area of garden that enabled us to trap him and he didn't scale the wall. The episode, scary as it was, proved an accelerated turning point in Ursu's relationship with us.

Not for the first time that day I somehow surpassed my natural physical strength and ran carrying Ursu's crate over the 120 foot distance to the summer house in a matter of seconds. Between us we manhandled him back into the crate and once again closed the crate door. Yet again he became totally calm within a fraction of a second. We then carried him back to the house and settled the crate in the office -the first time he'd ever entered a home. They say dogs can pick up scents from literally years before and it would be nice to think he inhaled good vibes from the histories of Lizzie and Daisy.

The dogs aren't fed much during travel because of travel sickness so I set about feeding Ursu by hand through the crate. Despite the baring of teeth and attempted biting only minutes before I thought it was important if we were to make progress together that we established right from the start that I wasn't scared of him. Hand feeding is also a form of bonding, and we certainly needed to do that. If I was scared he would also be scared, or alternatively he might see it as his chance to become dominant towards me and try and take over. Against the evidence of the last three hours I hung on to my instinct that Ursu was essentially a sweet dog, not a dominant one, and he needed to learn to relax through trust. His hunger got the better of him and he chose to risk feeding from my extended fingers through the bars and safety of his closed crate, snatching at the biscuits. We'd bought in quality dried food and not knowing how strong his constitution was it had always been our plan to feed him lightly and regularly in the first days. The experts say direct eye contact is threatening to a dog – in the wild it's seen as an aggressive act; likewise so is smiling, which, to a dog, is the equivalent of baring teeth. And Ursu, to all intents and purposes, was feral. So I fed him without directly looking at him, with my body turned away from him, and didn't speak.

So much for shaking hands on the deal that Ursu would be my primary responsibility. That evening my husband set to, erecting fencing on our stone patio immediately outside the doors to the office and putting straw down so that Ursu needn't be threatened with the sight of a collar or lead and could do his toilet and come straight back in. Whether he would opt to do this or simply soil the office we didn't know. What we soon learned was that his instincts told him the small area he was in, which was recognisable to him to some degree as 'home' and not overwhelmingly large, was his personal domain. Dogs don't soil their personal space given the choice and on his very first evening he opted to run outside for a quick pee and then straight back in. The straw was laid down for him so that he sensed this as outdoors and it might well have been used in Romania. We threw a treat into his crate to lead him back in and he went straight to it and we closed the gate again. Closing the gate on him was to become a big part of his first few weeks with us for both our benefits.

We then left him to sleep off his stress.

Let sleeping dogs lie - we put water in there when things had calmed down a bit

Attempting to talk to a dog that has barely ever been spoken to (and only then predominantly in a threatening style) would have been too much for him, especially amidst so many other novel and simultaneous sensory experiences. And in any event it would have been like rattling on in Double Dutch at a time when he was already stressed. The only word he knew was his name. So, to begin the slow progress of building mutual trust (I was as wary of him as he was of me), I decided to sleep on the old sofa in the office with him, directly in front of his crate about eight feet away. I settled down with a night light and didn't speak other than to say Ursu in a soft voice reassuringly maybe three or four times during the night. I wanted him to come to regard me as a stabilising non-threatening presence. I couldn't do this other than by being quiet and calm, and demanding nothing of him. I slept restlessly but made no sudden movements and whenever I sneaked a peek over his way he was looking back at me. It would have been the longest period of time he had ever spent in the company of one human being. Throughout the night I also heard him spending an interminable amount of time biting his nails. He would noisily chew for up to twenty minutes at a time, take a break of a couple of minutes and then start up all over again. Whether he'd acquired this activity as the only pathetic means of alleviating some of his boredom during the long lonely years or whether it was indicative of an unbalanced mental state, or simply that his nails were uncomfortably sharp and long through lack of exercise, we had yet to establish.

The next two months – getting to a baseline

There was no way we could pack Ursu up and take him to a dog trainer. He was feral. We were at a starting block way back from the normal start line. It was down to me, with the help of what I'd gleaned about dog psychology, to apply an innate understanding of his mind-set to try and win him over. One thing was for sure. My husband and I agreed that, whilst he needed our special care and attention, we weren't going to fall into the trap of treating him like an indulged child. It would do him no favours and simply feed his insecurities. Dogs need calm strong leaders in order to trust. And without trust he would neither relax nor begin to listen. He was a dog and needed to be treated like one, with the horrors of his past no reason to treat him as today's victim.

Day 1: 11th January 2015

   The next morning was truly special. We'd decided we weren't going to approach Ursu and panic him. It was for Ursu to come to us if and when he was ready. I'd anticipated that if ever this happened it wouldn't be for a long while. Ursu had decided to shut off completely. So for the foreseeable future, as far as we were concerned, if he only wanted to venture in and out of his crate - which he favoured as his safe sanctuary - for snatched toilet breaks then that was fine with us. We would be guided by him and by what he could cope with. He would set the pace. We couldn't afford to try and accelerate beyond his comfort zone as one step forward could lead to several steps back and worse, to a complete impasse. First thing on the Sunday morning I moved slowly and quietly towards his crate, conscious of his eyes on me the whole time, opened the gate and walked away from him without once looking at him. After about 10 minutes he came out of his crate, did a half-hearted tiny pee on the carpet and rushed back in where he settled back down to look at me. The first incredible thing to comment on here is that this was one of only a minor number of times in all the while he has lived with us that he has soiled indoors. And then, only as a nervous squirt of submissive behaviour, as dogs do this almost as homage to the more dominant force. It's a message that they're not going to try and take the other on. I'd learned from the volunteers that adult dogs are easier to toilet train than puppies for the simple fact that it's in a dog's instinct not to soil its own domain and with the added advantage of being able to control itself. Ursu surpassed all expectations. Despite, or maybe because of, having had to tolerate living amongst his and other dogs' faeces for years, we weren't called upon to house train him at all. He simply knew, given the configuration we'd set up for him, that he didn't have to soil his home. No training was involved.

Having retreated from his crate I decided to sit on the floor in front of the sofa opposite him and just busied myself with texts, careful all the while not to look at him. After a further five minutes of this non-confrontational set-up a remarkable thing happened. Ursu crept out, came and sat in front of me and looked me straight in the eye. With my phone to hand I snatched a quick shot and this will forever, I'm sure, be my all-time favourite photo of him. Those eyes say it all, and less than 24 hours in our care. Adjectives are superfluous.

If ever further evidence was required of a dog's strong emotional intelligence, this must surely cement the proof. A few seconds on from looking me in the eye he sat down and laid his head on my thigh and then lifted his head and averted his gaze – a dog signal of submission. And submission not through fear, but through a willingness to give things a go. Because in that instant he didn't trust. He had never belonged to anyone or lived in a home, or taken an instruction. He'd survived on his own wits and he wasn't going to surrender

that lightly. He was still a nervous dog with both of us and with much to learn. But at that moment I felt he instinctively knew to reward my belief that at heart he was a bright and good dog. He was saying that he was willing to take a chance. We would work together as a team.

One thing that came across on his very first day with us was that whilst jittery around us, he nevertheless wanted to be with us. I find it fascinating the way in which over the centuries the dog has become so connected with man as its natural pack leader that even one so badly abused for so great a length of time, the natural instinct was still to latch on to a human that appeared not to be intent on hurting him. Here was a dog that, apart from maybe occasional flashes of kindness from strangers, a tossed food fragment onto the streets for instance, knew only cruelty at the hands of humans. And yet his inherent instinct in this new and bewildering environment was to look to the human for his salvation.

Monica's Romanian Rescue had been eminently responsible in initially not letting a lay couple take on a dog like Ursu. It would have been quite the wrong thing to do to let an unpredictable canine go and live with a couple, no matter how well-intentioned, simply because the human had taken a fancy to its eyes. It had taken quite a bit of persuading to be allowed him. Underscoring the charity's responsible attitude towards its work, a volunteer made contact with me as early as mid-morning on the first day wanting to know how things were going and this contact remained regular for quite a while. There was no suggestion of dumping and forgetting. They wanted to know that matters were under control.

On the subject of control, we didn't want Ursu to swing from human aversion to separation anxiety – something that a dog that has been starved of love and care for so long can easily do, melting into the pleasurable excitement of finding someone that cares, and consequently being unable to cope with being solitary. Helping Ursu to control his behaviour was important. We established on the very first day that Ursu had just two behaviours, calm and blind panic, spiralling into the latter within a split second, triggered by absolutely anything from the sound of a voice, to a movement, or some imagined threat that only he was tuning in to. There's a picture of him here on his first afternoon with us, sat cross legged (I understand dogs do this for no other reason than for balance and that it isn't breed associated) looking chilled-out, if a little wary. Yet seconds later he was panicking. We have no idea what sparked it.

We decided that to control his world for him we needed to limit his space - something he was unused to and didn't know what to do with. So we created a barrier between the front and back of the office, using strategically placed furniture which became a permanent feature for a couple of months. The idea was that he was in a safe haven where he could associate with us but from afar. We weren't 'in his face'. Likewise, he couldn't run riot in a cavernous wilderness and panic himself in the process.

One thing he was seemingly naturally good at was coping with being ignored. Not attracting attention whilst in the shelter, with its inherent dangers, was a good day for him. We needed to play to the calm side of him before we could move forward, even when he showed signs of coming out of his shell, for both excitement and anxiety resulted in the same thing – blind panic. He simply didn't understand his new world and the good bits were bewildering. So, for the first couple of days we studiously avoided him whilst nevertheless being in very close proximity. We went quietly about our business sitting at our computers and would leave and re-enter the room without notice. All the time he would look at us, reading our language. What we were trying to say to him is that we were non-threatening protectors who were asking nothing of him. But likewise we were the pack leaders. We could go into his domain but he couldn't enter ours without invitation. During this time we did very little with him other than put small portions of dried food down for him twice a day, and let him out of the office onto the small patio to do his ablutions. On one of his trips outdoors in the evening he could hear a couple of dogs over a quarter of a mile away barking in the dark and he joined in as though he was part of their pack.

On the second night - which was at the end of his first full day with us - I again slept on the office sofa and was once more treated to a night of incessant nail baiting. And then began a daily rhythm of training delivered simply, quietly and consistently.

Day 4: 14th January 2015

Ursu had been with us just two and a half days and had spent his third night on his own downstairs in his own little shelter in the office. I'd placed an old T shirt in his crate to build-up the scent association. We hadn't heard a peep out of him all night and he greeted me enthusiastically as I walked into the room, standing up in his closed crate and wagging his tail. Whenever he was in his crate we would close the gate across for both his and our own protection. He visibly relaxed when the gate was closed and not knowing what we would be greeted with were we to leave him to his own devices overnight it felt the sensible thing to do. As I opened his crate he came out, followed me and lent his body into me in a C curve. Dogs can do this for a variety of reasons, from trying to seek protection, to demonstrating affection, through to trying to dominate. The last explanation, I liked to think, could be dismissed and my heart glowed to think that he was already willing to try and bond with me and had been pleased to reunite with me. My husband and I had concluded before Ursu's arrival that only I would attempt to handle Ursu in the first instance, and then only at Ursu's instigation. But my husband was very much a quiet and present force and had spent his birthday the day before in the pouring rain creating a bigger Colditz-style escape-proof recreation area for Ursu that he could begin his rehabilitation in. Overlooking the garden it afforded Ursu the luxury of becoming familiar with the outdoors behind the safety of a mesh fence which he was familiar with from his shelter days.

As early as Day 2 we had started calling Ursu Nelson and he picked it up within minutes, probably because it was one of only a handful of words we ever used with him. He had

barely been spoken to in all his life and then only in Romanian and we therefore kept words to the minimum to minimise stress and potential panic. We alternated between Ursu and Nelson and he showed no signs of confusion, if anything he seemed to relish communication. Animal experts say you can talk to a dog in any language – it's all the same to them. It's the tone of voice that spells out to them what the message intent is.

The pattern of our days would begin with me letting him out onto the patio to do his toilet and then I would put his food down for him in his section of the office and leave him to enjoy it. He ate his breakfast – always in five seconds flat - listening to Radio 4's The Today Programme. I would put this on at low volume lulling him into the belief that unfamiliar male and female voices alike didn't necessarily mean danger. Had he understood the content he might have thought otherwise.

Ursu, because of his history, would become over-excited by food and would start running around and jumping up and down and squealing at the mere sight of his bowl. He had only ever survived through scavenging in the streets and being thrown small morsels of tasteless dry food, much of it hard-fought for. He has a four inch deep scar immediately under his left eye, no doubt having come off worse in a scrap with another dog. Likewise he has a broken front fang and various missing teeth along the bottom row. We can't be sure how and when these injuries occurred but pictorial evidence suggests it was at Cornetu where the dogs can do nothing but fight one another for survival. Maybe the badly discoloured dark brown teeth snapped off through malnourishment, or at the hands of human brutality. They were certainly filthy. The now-healed eye wound is so deep that it must have been very painful at the time and, feeling both starved and wretched, he wouldn't have received any veterinary treatment or comfort, all of this on top of a brutal castration without anaesthetic.

For a dog that had never luxuriated in the warmth and comfort of a home, he took to it with surprising alacrity. Many rescue dogs observe proffered comforts with caution and disbelief. Not so Ursu. He was frightened of open space but took to home comforts as though things had never been any different. He already had an understanding of crates and had been in one as recently as his travels from Romania. This new one was simply a comfier one with blankets. But surprisingly he didn't need introducing to his day bed - he saw it and simply took up residence.

Unfortunately, he adopted the same sense of entitlement over our old sofa and chairs. Well, to be realistic, they were in his domain area which he had quickly called 'home' so it's not surprising he claimed them as his. He's a bright dog. But we're not comfortable with animals on furniture and beds (we're all different about our house rules, it's a personal thing), added to which Ursu was a dog that hadn't been socialised and didn't understand boundaries. He was just as likely to jump onto tables as we introduced him to wider parts of the home. We'd introduced the old furniture as part of his socialising training. My husband and I had been sitting on these chairs whilst in his company and it was too soon to think he could call the shots whilst still otherwise pretty much feral, assuming he

had first claim on the seating. He was also an exceptionally hairy dog that hadn't been groomed in over seven years and had consequently developed a particularly heavy coat to help withstand the harsh winters of Romania, made all the more unappealing by an unkempt whiff. He would quite boldly jump up onto the sofa and make himself comfy. We tackled it by saying 'no' in a neutral but non-negotiable way and by pushing his hind quarters gently and saying 'off'. He'd snap at us but get down after a second or third push and quickly came to understand the score – maybe within a couple of days – but would continue to ignore the understood command and continue his snapping as we made body contact.

The natural instinct when a dog snaps at you is to recoil, which tells the dog it has won. We felt it important that we 'won' on this one or else Ursu might start to create havoc on more important issues assuming 'top dog' status. So we persisted with the counter-intuitive action of touching him again, after a warning snap from him, but not harshly. After about a week he stopped taking us on and instead developed the cunning habit of jumping onto the furniture when we weren't in the room (we could see through a glass door that he did this within seconds of our departure) and jumping off the second we re-appeared. We ignored this behaviour other than to say 'good boy' as he jumped off and he very gradually gave up the trick in his own time, in his own way, without a second of unpleasantness from us. As we finally opened up the house to him he made no attempt to re-introduce his devilment. The rule had become embedded in his own little house and he carried this through to the rest of our home, which by the time he was introduced to it, bit by bit, he had come to regard as his domain too with the respect that a dog shows for its own environment. But this was an early sign to us that the basic nature of this dog was one of entitlement and that he wasn't going to be as naturally biddable as our two previous dogs. This dog had a mind of its own which wasn't a great surprise. For how otherwise could he have survived for so long? Yet this small and relatively harmless early defiance accompanied by snapping teeth reinforced to us that we needed to be sure he could trust and respect us before opening up his boundaries. Only by deciding for himself that he was willing to relinquish his stance and start to open his mind to instructions, could we ever contemplate introducing him to the wider world. We were prepared to wait.

One habit he introduced within two days of joining us was a strong urge to mouth my hands on greeting me in the mornings. My husband was very much against this as we have young grandchildren and a niece and we had a tacit agreement between us that whilst the majority of the time we are at home by ourselves - and we understood that this might be a dog that never progressed to being socialised beyond our walls - nevertheless we didn't want a dog that might harm a child under our roof.

Mouthing is a bonding activity between a puppy and its mother, with the mother eventually letting its offspring know that enough is enough and it should now stop. We weren't sure of Ursu's age – he looked younger than nine but his tracked history meant he couldn't be less than seven – and yet here he was, a grown dog, wanting to bond like puppy to Mum. I felt it was so sad that he had been denied this, as surely he would have been, at puppy stage. Many strays in Romania quickly become separated from their Mums through tough street survival and are robbed of the crucial formative early weeks when the bitch teaches them how to be a dog. Ursu had had to learn to get by on his own, belonging to no-one and nowhere, and it melted my heart that he was now doing what he had been denied the chance of doing years back. His primitive instinct at the first chance to bond with something was to adopt puppy behaviour. I didn't want to discourage him from bonding with me – it was vital that we formed a connection if we were to live harmoniously together - and if this was his instinctive way of telling me I was becoming the leader then that was fine with me. So every morning for about three weeks the first thing he wanted to do on our reunion was do small harmless 'bites' on my hands. He did these relatively gently for a dog that was just as happy gnashing his teeth aggressively over something he took a dislike to. I would gently stroke his head whilst he did it, praying that something imaginary didn't startle him into panic, as was the pattern of his behaviour, leaving me with broken bleeding skin. It would have been a deal breaker for my husband. After the three weeks, whenever he attempted to mouth my hands, I would just walk away from him and ignore him – replicating how a bitch would teach its young that now was the time to stop and start growing up. I progressed to saying 'no' and walking away, only introducing sound when I knew he wouldn't be startled by the noise. As a result 'no' was a word he quickly came to learn through his mouthing and jumping onto furniture activities. The mouthing ceased naturally and we were able to introduce 'no' as a message to other behaviours, which could be delivered in the same non-aggressive, neutral tone.

Day 5: 15th January

As well as mastering his alternative name very quickly, within just a couple of days Ursu was answering to 'sit', 'stay' and 'come here' and was regularly praised as 'Good Boy'. 'Sit' he associated with his bowl being put down for him. As he naturally sat, so we would say 'sit' and after a couple of times he sat on command, but only in relation to food and treats. He didn't sit just because we randomly asked him to. We kept it simple to begin with. 'Come here' was said more upbeat and I would tap my leg and he instinctively knew what I meant. 'Stay' was said with a hand held up signalling stop and if he moved towards us I would say 'no' and repeat 'stay' with the same hand movement. We said 'Good Boy' each time he did something that we asked.

Everything was uttered 'sotto voce'. Ursu simply didn't like noise. The experts say if you shout at a dog its interpretation is that you are out of control and therefore not worthy of its respect. Similarly, talk to a dog in a baby voice and it considers you inadequate and not up to the job of leadership. Neutral and clear is the perceived best way to communicate with a dog which makes sense to me. Yet this didn't work with Ursu. It scared him. We were right to have anticipated that he needed a quiet and calm environment because not only did volume of noise unhinge him, only in such an exceptionally still place could I be audible to him in a tone delivered literally just a notch above a whisper. But in speaking to him quietly it was also important that I didn't sound as though I were negotiating with him, but, rather, communicating a command. He responded well in the main and wasn't fazed by the normal chatter between husband and wife that he wasn't party to. But if ever I momentarily forgot and talked directly to him in a normal non-confrontational tone he would start panicking.

Ursu also showed signs of wanting to play – an excellent sign that he had the makings of a balanced dog in him and something to be encouraged. But the encouragement to be a happy dog had to be managed as he was still flipping within an instant from perky to panic-stricken. He liked chasing my slippers and plunging his teeth into them whilst I was wearing them. We needed to keep our own bodies out of the dynamics or someone was going to get hurt. So we dropped a tennis ball on the floor and he immediately picked it up in his mouth and toyed with it for a few minutes before losing interest. He was learning how to play on his own and knew what to do with a ball. Not a big thing in itself but some rescue dogs, particularly those that have been incarcerated for a significant period of time, have no idea what a toy is when given one and just ignore it. What's more, others are so sad their tails are constantly down. The remedy for this I'm told is to hold the tail up and

45

eventually the dog's mood lifts to match the mood of its tail. No need for this with Ursu. His pom-pom spitz-like tail was regularly up, albeit matted and filthy.

Ursu's tail as it is today

His nails still held a fascination for him and he continued with his ritual of chewing them for hours at a time. We still weren't sure of the motivation, painful length or just an acquired behaviour to alleviate bore-dom, but he didn't seem to be doing himself any harm and whilst ever his movements involved just mooching about on carpet with only quick dashes outside and back, I didn't feel there was a threat of his nails getting pushed back up into his paws causing pain and complications. So we let him get on with it for the time being, grating as the sound was.

There was no way we could approach Ursu with a collar and lead. Much to our surprise he'd arrived from Romania sporting a blue collar but it was so loose that he'd slipped it within hours of his arrival and I suspect it had been dropped on over his head more as a gesture than anything else. Some weeks later we returned it amongst a variety of provisions driven out to Romania and I'm sure its next owner treated it with greater respect. The overwhelming majority of strays are friendly and biddable, and only too pleased to be amongst humans.

Whenever I so much as walked anywhere within Ursu's vicinity carrying either collar or lead, even though I wasn't actually attempting to try and engage with him, he would start screaming and running around. We didn't want this safe harbour of his to become associated with bad things and so when he was distracted by his food, or simply looking out of the window, I would nonchalantly place both on the floor in some haphazard fashion not relating to anything, other than for a treat next to it. He clocked it and desperately wanted tasty foods he'd never devoured before in his life, but wouldn't go near it. Rather than leave the collar and lead there indefinitely, which didn't really teach him anything, instead after some minutes I would recover both the collar and the lead and put the treat away. He's a bright dog and worked out that if he wasn't prepared to go up to the collar and lead the treat would be taken away again. By the fourth day of doing this matter-of-factly two or three times a day without trying to engage with him in any way - and keeping the activity isolated from meal times and anything else – he worked up the nerve to quickly run up to the offending items, snatch the treat, and run away again. Once again, he'd taken the decision himself without duress and it resulted in a tasty morsel and praise for his actions.

Treats are the natural product to use in training a dog. The dog does what it's asked to do and it gets a treat. The association builds, and eventually the dog executes the command on voice only. It's a well-known technique. Treats worked for Ursu with the collar and lead because there was no instruction involved. He simply 'nicked' some food when he thought the coast was clear. 'Sit' worked because it was a simple and natural thing for Ursu to do and he then associated this with seeing his bowl lowered to the floor. But in absolutely every other form of training treats were counter-productive - he either became so overexcited by food that he couldn't focus on learning and screened me out, or he was so confused by the instruction that he spiralled into feeling terrified and food held no appeal. I had to think 'outside the box' about just about everything.

Day 6: 16th January

Our house is accessed down a long drive with the garden to the front of the house and with a strip of lawn down the side of the office which also looks out over the driveway. Our office overlooking the garden was spot on for Ursu as he was able to take in all the novel sights – rabbits, squirrels, doves, wandering neighbours' cats – with us for company and from the safety of his home. The downside was that delivery vans were also clearly in his sight and he would go ballistic at them. White vans and red postal vans got him really agitated and he would bark through the glass at them quite viciously. I've heard stories where many strays take months to find their voice. Ursu located his on day one. At this point of our relationship I don't think it was a guard dog reaction but one of sheer terror. Vans reminded him of dog catchers. If we spotted a van before he did we would stand in front of him commanding his space and put a hand up and say 'stay'. This was about as effective as a chocolate fire guard in the early days but we persevered and he has gradually, and I stress gradually, calmed down. He still barks but it's as a guard dog alert to us, rather than in fear, and in truth can be quite helpful. We know that psychologically it isn't ideal for him to see approaching vehicles, but the configuration of the house demands it. To him we are putting him on the front line and so he does what he thinks we are asking him to do in the circumstances – take charge. But then, quite rightly, he doesn't know how to execute what he thinks is his responsibility and things get out of hand. Over time he's become quieter and, rather like when we humans on a rocky flight nervously glance at the cabin crew taking our cue from them as to whether we should be worried - translating their nonchalance as a sign we can relax - so Ursu has come to regard my husband and I as the unflappable crew who are in charge. If we are OK then things must be alright. He's also narrowed and redefined his boundaries and no longer joins in with the barking of neighbouring dogs.

Day 7: 17th January

A whole week with us and what a week! Ursu is my main priority from waking up in the morning until going to bed at night and each day we keep to the same routine, limited that it is. Because Ursu has never experienced electricity and it's currently the winter months, he's dead on his feet by 6.00 p.m. and wanting to settle for the night. In Romania his habits will have followed natural light and darkness. So we are currently working to this and in time he'll gradually adjust to longer hours. Naturally we want access to the office beyond 6.00 p.m. so we just go about our business whilst he snoozes in his crate that he favours at this time of night and we're sure to enable a toilet break about 8.00 p.m.

He's coping with the office 'phone ringing. He barks at people even before they get as far as the front door so the ringing of the doorbell doesn't elicit any additional objections from Ursu.

Earlier today my husband put the TV on that's at a height on the wall in the office, without the sound turned up and he and Ursu watched the horse racing together. He's never seen a TV before and it's possible he's never seen a horse before and he was mesmerised, possibly wondering why mammoth dogs were racing round with a body on their backs. In any event he didn't bark so that's quite a breakthrough. He also let me take a snatched look at his teeth. When I say 'let' I did it very quickly before he'd had the chance to realise. The second he cottoned on he pulled away but he didn't attempt to bite me. His teeth are still a dreadful colour but the dental sticks are starting to make a slight difference. I don't think they get optimum time to work because Ursu simply swallows them in a nanosecond.

Day 8: 18th January

Ursu has progressed to sleeping with his collar and lead on the floor of his crate during the day and is gradually relaxing around the sight of it. Now I no longer close the gate on his crate when he opts to go in there during the day although we still close it at night. The closing of the gate is a signal to him that he need not worry about anything until he next sees us when we will take over again. During the day he's building up his confidence taking in the world looking through the office glass and with one of us always around to see off a marauding aggressor, such as a floating leaf. I don't leave the collar in his crate overnight for obvious safety reasons. He backed off again when he saw me holding it today but the screaming has abated and he'll hopefully let us know when he's ready. I think he's taken over the training regime.

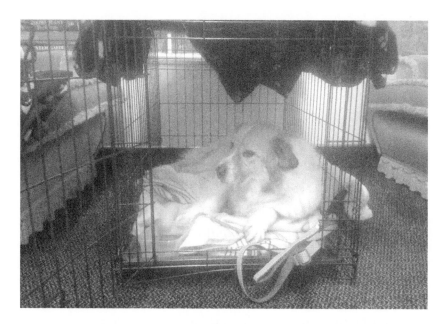

Today I forgot to close the barrier between his side of the office and ours and he slipped through but retreated to his side when I pointed and said 'go back'. So he's now starting to understand another instruction and it's important that all this socialising is learned in his small confine, much as I'm tempted to let him roam further. It will then be the natural state of things when his boundaries are relaxed. Who knows, we may be able to introduce him to other people one fine day.

Day 9: 19th January

Today got off to a bad start and it was my fault. I introduced him to the collar again before I'd given him his breakfast. My rationale was that as he's keen for his food first thing in the morning and knows he's going to get something maybe I could use this moment to momentarily touch some part of his body with the collar whilst he was focused on food and gradually he would become desensitised. His reaction taught me just how damaged this dog is.

Ursu is literally giddy with excitement in the mornings when we reunite. It's as though he can't quite believe he's still with us – another day – another day in his new life. I should have known not to try and introduce something new when he wasn't at his calmest, even allowing for the fact that his excitement was glee. He went into his usual over-excited state at the sight of food and became confused by the sight of the collar, which by his reckoning wasn't part of the deal. It underscored to me how new activities need to be introduced in bite sizes with no two things happening simultaneously as he simply can't handle it. He became very nervous and started to pee (an act of submission) against the old chair, stopping mid-flow when I said 'no'. Bless him. All my fault. His fear is omnipresent, his permanent companion. The only way forward is slow, slow, slow.

Later in the day he allowed the window cleaner to do his job without barking at him or his van. This required some skulduggery. My husband has started to join in with the interactions with Ursu, but still it's only ever one of us at a time so as not to overpower him. My husband fed him treats throughout the duration telling him 'wait' and then 'yes' when he could take the treat. Ursu snatched at each scrap at the first opportunity, table manners aren't his strong point, but all in all it was a good moment knowing my husband plus food was enough to keep Ursu's eyes and brain focused on the treats and not the man making a noise with running water against the windows. Even two days ago this wouldn't have happened. Slow as it is Ursu moves forward bit by bit every single day.

I've bought him a pillow case holder in the shape of a lion for something to stimulate him and play with during this sedentary time. I sneaked a treat inside it and he worked out the mechanics within seconds, but then accessing food in record time does appear to be one of his most impressive skills. What's nice is that now Lion is lacking a treat he'll nevertheless voluntarily pick it up and play with it again. He's really getting the hang of this toy = play lark.

He's also learnt 'down' today in less than a day – taught to him in a whisper and by patting the floor. He's definitely smart. I always try and remember to say his name before speaking to him unlike how we normally interact with humans when we often tag the name on at the end. All my words to him are novel and I need to first arrest his attention so it's not just a lot of white noise to him.

Day 10: 20th January

I drove my car up the drive, stopping outside of the office and Ursu watched me intently through the glass whilst I unloaded a large shop. He didn't make a sound. He'd recognised and differentiated the sound of my motor from other vehicles from 200 yards away. And he can't have heard it more than a couple of times.

Day 11: 21st January

It's snowing here today and Ursu is making it clear he doesn't like the wet and cold and would rather snuggle down inside. I heard a story of another Romanian stray rehomed in the UK that would lie down and curl up if the weather turned bad whilst out on a walk. Self-preservation instincts. How Ursu survived outdoors through all those freezing wet winters of

Romania I don't know. He must have been miserable, although he had developed one of the thickest coats I've ever seen on a dog to help compensate.

We think his thick coat is responsible for his survival in more ways than one. The dog catchers, as well as poisoning the dogs with anti-freeze causing a slow painful death, chuck freezing cold water over them in sub-zero temperatures causing the thinner coated dogs to perish from hypothermia. I've heard the volunteer women wear sunglasses when they enter the shelters to hide their tears and minimise the mocking from the staff.

Just before he joined us we'd researched his looks and thought that within his mishmash of breeds there was a trace of Carpathian Shepherd (Romanian Sheepdog), albeit he was much smaller in size. The temperament of the Carpathian Shepherd dog is good manners, courage and devotion and the breed is said to battle bears, if needed, to protect its master and its flock. No bears here I'm glad to say, but he has gone on to develop a protective streak which was to come out a few days later and over alcohol of all things.

With such a heavy coat we were surprised that Ursu had taken a dislike to the relatively mild winter weather conditions of the UK, but after years of draughts and wet shelters he must have built up an aversion to them. Cold is one thing and most dogs' coats will naturally thicken to keep their body temperatures up, but constant wet bedding combined with howling wind isn't good for their health and Ursu's mental association with our change in weather conditions was an uncomfortable one.

The collar problem. We really did want to wait until Ursu was ready to take his collar, but actually putting a collar on a dog is something the human has to do; a dog can't do it for *itself or rationalise what it's all about. So we began to wonder how we were ever going to progress. Ursu had established his rules with us over the collar and there was no added association we knew of that we could introduce to make the next step of putting one on him attractive to him. The collar was now in his crate and on the floor without a reaction from him but that was as far as we could go, even with treats to hand. We'd reached an impasse and were concerned that the longer we left it the less we would be able to progress on everything else still to come.*

It's simply not feasible to have a pet dog that isn't wearing a collar or taking a lead unless you happen to live in the middle of nowhere. So we decided to bite the bullet and manhandle him as gently as we could and simply get the collar on him. I can't tell you how apprehensive we were. Looking back and knowing Ursu as he is today it's hard to believe that the prospect of getting a collar on a dog was both frightening and daunting. But then there aren't many of us who will willingly

handle a dog we know will bite us in its fear. We wanted the manoeuvre to be as seamless as possible and spent quite a bit of time choreographing our individual moves. As Ursu's main relationship was with me it was agreed that my husband would stand the other side of his barricaded thigh-height domain with treats in his hand. I would stand behind Ursu in his shelter and whilst he was distracted by the food and focused on my husband, I would manhandle him into the collar. He's not a huge dog but at around 17 kilos (as we later came to establish), and with a very determined attitude, we knew it wouldn't be easy. And I didn't know his exact collar size as I couldn't get near to this part of his body, let alone brandishing anything as threatening looking as a piece of string or a tape measure. The first thing we did was both don a pair of gloves. The puncture holes in my husband's gloves acquired the day Ursu arrived with us served as a salutary reminder that we couldn't leave anything to chance. We chose mid-morning as the time of day. He'd breakfasted and wouldn't be expecting food and it was daytime bright light – small details but the little things could make all the difference. I'd deliberately bought a relatively narrow, soft, clip-on collar. I stood behind him waiting for my chance. When he was holding his head at the exact right angle to receive a treat from my husband I zoomed in, and clipped it shut in two seconds flat. He flinched but then relaxed and I took my hands away before he could contemplate a warning snap or snarl. He got his treat.

Day 12: 22nd January

My yesterday's guess as to how tight I should make Ursu's collar without scaring him into thinking he was being throttled wasn't too accurate. Each morning he seeks affection but I'm *only allowed to stroke his head and the top portion of his back. His neck area or any suggestion of physically containing him is out of bounds. I'd taken a guess making the circumference smaller than the blue collar he'd arrived in which he slipped on Day 1. He slipped today's collar too – he has the knack of just pushing it off with his front paw from the back of his head – quite an art. So we went back to the drawing board with the same pantomime as the day before and once again he became a dog with a collar.*

In the afternoon a male friend with a low-key non-threatening energy about him visited. He entered Ursu's domain but studiously ignored him. After about an hour my friend proffered a treat to Ursu which he quickly snatched and then rushed to hide behind me. A great advancement. Ursu hadn't screamed the house down and, more significantly, demonstrated that he was beginning to see me as his protector, even though I'd done the dastardly deed of putting him in a collar. Advancing towards regarding me as his leader is just the thing we need.

He continues to answer to both Ursu and Nelson but since he's the only animal we're addressing it's probably not overly significant in terms of his intelligence levels on a broader dimension. Still, it helps embed his identity.

Day 15: 25th January

During this early morning's cuddle, which we conduct both sat on the floor together, Ursu started to groom me as well as himself, small licks of my hand in that long repetitive rhythm synonymous with ablutions rather than love or enjoying the taste. He continues to mouth my hands – I started weaning him off this at three weeks but now, two weeks in, he's including me in his grooming routine too.

Later in the day he allowed me for the first time to hold his head briefly and very loosely whilst we did 'stay', and 'come here', which I rewarded with a treat. Whether he'd taken the decision to think that as we didn't hurt him when we put the collar on then maybe we wouldn't hurt him ever, I don't know, but he does appear to have relaxed another notch. Interestingly, now it's on he's not in the least bit bothered by it, although he's still disturbed when he sees me pick up the lead so I continue to do just that. He's OK with it as a non-moving object in his crate, but it's seeing me doing something with it that distresses him. So I lift it up and place it back down again just as quickly, before his mind spirals. I repeat this action regularly throughout the day, occasionally dropping a treat by it. I want Ursu to start to regard the lead as no big deal with little significance. It's just an inanimate object, same as the furniture is.

Day 16: 26th January

Ursu is starting to accept our gardener who comes a couple of mornings a week, barking at him through the glass from the safety of indoors, but willing to cease if I am with him. He even accepted a treat from the 80 year-old whilst they were both sat outdoors on the enclosed patio, but from a significant distance away, causing the gardener to stretch out his arm to him. Ursu snatched the treat and ran to sit behind me, as he did on his first encounter with the first male to have visited.

Day 17: 27th January

In his excitement at the prospect of breakfast (Ursu literally starts jumping up and down in the air and running around in circles), he accidentally knocked over the barrier between his half and our half of the office. I came back to find him sitting in his side of the room looking out for me. He'd made no attempt to venture further into the house. Bless him. He picks up instantly what it is we are asking him to do, though he's not always prepared to do it.

Day 18: 28th January

Oh dear. The human has made another mistake. I let Ursu out of the office door without realising the gate onto the lawn was open. I was terrified that just two and a half weeks on from joining us he would do a repeat bolt. In my haste to get to him I slipped on the snow. He was using his freedom to have a pee against a chosen tree and in that time my husband was able to get to him and he responded to a treat whilst I gently and gingerly put a finger around his collar. My husband picked him up and carried him back to the house. So whilst I made a bad mistake and luck was once again on our side - as there's no doubt in my mind that once his ablutions were over he would have begun tearing down the drive on that auto instinct of his to run, run, run - the incident did teach me that whilst he's nervous, he's lost none of a dog's basic instinct to investigate his surroundings. What's more, he let me momentarily touch his collar and my husband pick him up without putting up a struggle. Maybe once a dog's feet are off the ground it senses its vulnerability and the logic of staying still, as he did when the driver deposited him in the back of our car the day we picked him up.

59

Although he eventually did give this up, two and a half weeks in and he's still including the sofa as part of his agility circuit as he does his twice-daily celebratory and highly excited mad charging around the office on sight of his next meal. We're still playing safe and only giving him small portions of quality dried food but the monotony does nothing to quell his sheer thrill at being fed, yet again. Eighteen days, some 20 plus meals in and he still behaves as though he can't quite believe someone feeds him.

We're starting to randomly leave the gate barrier between his side and our side of the office open from time to time with the door leading into the rest of the house ajar too and he doesn't venture through. You might ask is this mean, does it really matter, but we really need him to acquiesce to the seemingly trivial commands before we can introduce him to the commands that any socialised dog needs for a balanced and full life. If he will listen and obey then his life can broaden, and with it he'll come to relish more freedom and joy.

Snow and thunder overnight and like an alert Mum I was listening out for him from my bedroom upstairs, but not a sound from him all night. Howling winds and extreme weathers, thunder and lightning. He must have endured them all. But then he was alone, cold and wet, and outdoors in the thick of it. By comparison, tucked up in the relative warmth, dry as toast and in the security of his gated crate, he must have felt he was in heaven.

Day 19: 29th January

I've been toying with buying a harness lead – many experts recommend them over a standard lead for those dogs nervous *of the traditional method. But I'm still not confident that Ursu will let me handle his body. So instead I decided to have another go with the standard lead and, waiting for my moment, I successfully clipped it on in a split second. I was treated to growling through bared teeth and a snap for my efforts but I instantly chucked Ursu his lion toy to play with.*

He soon became oblivious to the lead but as you might know, he wasn't going to let me get near it again to detach it. So I waited until he was lying down and relaxed and I exceptionally quickly unclipped it before he knew what I was up to, and left it on the floor for a few minutes before putting it away. My manual dexterity has improved enormously since we got this dog - sheer survival instincts.

By the afternoon he was letting me attach and detach the lead outside on the patio but became stressed when we were in a small enclosed corner area and was pulling and straining. We got through it one way or another and then repeated the whole thing a second time in a more open space.

I've started leaving his packet of treats on a work surface in the office and he doesn't attempt to get at them. Very impressive!

Day 20: 30th January

Regression. Ursu today is having none of the lead training. Won't let me anywhere near him with it. I decided not to push it and gave him the day off, turning my attentions to something else. Knowing that he's reasonably bright and not getting enough exercise right now I bought him a dog puzzle dinner tray to help stimulate him. Lots of trays which, if the dog can work out how to pull out the sections, reveals dry food. I showed him how it worked and he watched intently – food is his favourite subject – and he did OK with it, managing to open most of the drawers and devouring the kibble. But then he peed against the furniture - a sure sign of stress and submission. He did this once before on a training session he didn't understand and it's another little reminder to me not to expect too much too soon.

Day 21: 31st January

I've realised where I've been going wrong with the lead training. After deftly clipping the lead on I've been asking Ursu to come to me in order to be rewarded with a treat, the lead outstretched between us with he and I facing one another. To encourage him to walk for the fun of it I've been making the mistake of continuing to walk backwards whilst maintaining the treat held out to him in the hope that it will keep him moving towards me and get him used to the apparatus between us. But from a dog's viewpoint why would he do this? The instruction wasn't clear or finite enough for him at this stage and the reward was moving away from him, not towards him. All very confusing. I decided to adopt a different tack and outside on the patio, with him on the lead, I asked him to come to me by saying 'Ursu, come here' whilst staying stock still and holding out the treat. As he reached me I asked him to 'sit' at which point he got the reward. Just a tiny adjustment that might seem neither here nor there, but a significant shift in a dog's understanding.

By taking the instruction down to one component the lead became irrelevant. It just happened to be there but wasn't part of my interaction with him. He could ignore it and simply come to me and get a reward for doing so. Dogs are logical and think simply. Result! We did it just twice and then he became edgy. But twice was great. A breakthrough. And another lesson to me to think like a dog, not as a human. The lead means nothing to Ursu except that he's beginning to trust me not to hurt him with it. It's just something the human feels the need to place on him, but does not in itself at this stage represent anything he can relate to in a positive way.

Day 22: 1st February

Ursu barked lightly at the Sunday paper boy from the safety of his covered and closed crate but he stopped when I came into his room, as though he simply wanted to convey a warning to us. This bodes well that he will learn to accept us as the leaders of the pack but it's still very early days.

Today we had a fabulous time together with lead training. Ursu actually sat peacefully in front of me to have his lead put on – previously he would sometimes roll onto his back to block my access to his collar. For some reason he's happier about my putting it on than taking it off. Maybe because putting it on he now relates to getting a treat, whereas I've not introduced a positive association to taking it off. I can also attach it more cleanly and noiselessly than I can on removing it and Ursu is unnerved by sudden noise of any kind. Whatever Ursu's thinking might be I am going to introduce treats for both manoeuvres and if he starts getting porky with all these titbits and no exercise, well, it's all in a good cause and only a temporary problem. Many websites suggest using exceptionally yummy irresistible treats for dogs such as liver treats, sausages and cheese. Not so with Ursu. The plainest of biscuit could get him in a frenzy of excitement. Anything more tasty and we'd have had a complete disaster on our hands. It's impossible to expect a dog to concentrate on what you're asking it to do when it's drooling at the mouth and running amok in uncontrollable anticipation.

I tried the dinner tray with pockets again today and his solution was to grab it by its rope and throw it up in the air, snatching the food from the trays as they fell open on landing. I've washed it and am taking it to the charity shop for a furry friend with less lateral thinking, or at least greater patience.

I spent my first night alone with Ursu today and I admit to having been feeling very apprehensive. With no-one to look out for me should he turn nasty, I made doubly sure he didn't have any escape routes out of the office and I spent the evening well away from him in another room. I was pleased to have my husband home again the following evening.

Interestingly, when my husband got back we sat together on the old sofa in Ursu's area to chat. We must have stayed there a couple of hours chewing the cud over a glass of wine, the longest time we'd sat there, as previously we'd only parked ourselves on the seats for a few minutes at a time.

Apart from racing onto and off the sofa in his pre-meal excitement, Ursu had pretty much got the not going onto furniture rule sorted by this time. But after we left the room I twice had to shoo Ursu off the sofa. A three seater, he'd opted to jump up and curl himself into the exact spot on the sofa where my husband and I had been sitting. Each time I told him off he would get back on onto the same area my husband and I had sat. I guess he wanted to be part of the pack, or maybe he wanted to override our scent with his own. Whatever the exact reason, it was a direct response to my husband and me having sat there for an extended period.

Days 23 - 24: 2nd - 3rd February

Ursu loves playing with another new soft toy we've given him and is learning 'drop' allowing me to pick the toy up when I want to. This is an excellent sign that he's not going to be over possessive of his possessions and food. He soon gets tired and needs to sleep off the experience, but then he's not had a walk for over three years and is clearly unfit. Mental stimulation is also tiring for dogs and he must be feeling like he's at University. I keep all specific training to about ten minutes just twice a day. In fact everything happening to Ursu right now constitutes as training and he's clearly up for it but finding it knackering.

Just after me saying that Ursu understands the 'do not jump onto furniture' rule, the little rascal has regressed into taking a fancy to jumping onto the sofa and chairs again so I've covered them. Saves on stress and argument and the theory is that by the time we open up the remainder of the house he'll have gone so long without access to furniture that it will no longer occur to him to think it's anything related to him. I believe he's doing it because his confidence is growing bit by bit and he's flexing his muscles and testing us out.

We're trying to introduce him to the outdoors gradually. As a dog he's clearly curious to be out there but at the same time the open space causes him anxiety. But today was lovely and sunny and so I took him out onto his patio and left him for a short period entirely on his own for the very first time. He was there less than 10 minutes, while all the time he could see me in the office through the glass. With his barricaded mesh walls giving him a feeling of security and the sun easing his spirit, he lay down outside for the first time ever, on his side, no less, and did a bit of sunbathing. Until today he's always sat up ready for action, even with me by his side.

Day 25: 4th February

The male friend who met Ursu for the first time on Day 12 visited for a second time today. Ursu was a little more relaxed and friendlier with him than on the first occasion but not totally trusting. He took exception to my friend walking from the office into the main house and let out a single bark as if questioning his right to be in the property.

At midnight Ursu started barking from his crate. We still close it at night and it still has a permanent blanket over the top allowing a single view through the front, deeper into the office. When I came downstairs and joined him, but without opening his crate, he immediately stopped, yet when I left again he howled. So I let him out of his crate, calmed him by stroking him and gave him the chance to do his toilet outdoors which he didn't need. There's a school of thought that humans shouldn't appease a dog as, in the dog's mind, we're simply reaffirming that it's right to think there's something to be worried about. Comforting a dog simply feeds its anxiety. But it felt the right thing to do at the time and I'd remembered as I'd returned home late that evening that there had been a car accident less than a quarter of a mile from our home. No doubt Ursu was hearing the aftermath clear-up and it spooked him. He just needed to know I was around to protect him. Bless. He soon settled again.

Day 27: 6th February

Had a lovely time today videoing Ursu reasonably relaxed on his lead on a small patch of our garden. He wasn't sure what it was all about and why we were doing it. He has no concept of walking simply for the enjoyment of it. How sad is that? This is a dog that can flee for his life but doesn't understand why we are on the lawn together mooching around in a mellow way. He was looking a bit confused and it was only for a few seconds that he would move whilst on his lead before straining or sitting back down again, but the progress in just four weeks from an unapproachable dog to this was incredible and beautifully heart-warming. Posting the snippet to Monica's Facebook page was an uplifting feeling. So many people have invested so much of their time and patience in giving this dog its one chance and Ursu has grabbed it. What a resilient and intelligent hound. Later the same day my good friend of 99 years old came down for tea and Ursu took to her instantly.

Day 28: 7th February

Deciding to build on Ursu's sunbathing experience on the patio just three days before and a developing confidence, my husband and I left him there to walk together away from him about 40 yards down the drive to our garage, all the time remaining in full view. Alas the distance was too much for his nerves. He began barking and racing back and forth across the patio, desperately searching for a way back into the house, not a way to get to us. He couldn't handle the open space on his own, even though he could see us. Although our reaction to his wild behaviour, which was to straight away return to him, looked like it was he who was calling the shots - a supposed no-no between dog and master - his behaviour was agitated blind panic and not manipulation. He instantly calmed. Dogs live in the present. His present was scaring him and the sooner it ended the better it would be for him. This dog needs special care.

Later that afternoon, not wanting a fear of the outside to take deeper root with him, I put Ursu on his lead, threw caution to the wind and actually ran him up and down the side of the office on the grass with me. That he was prepared to do this alongside me amazed me. Maybe because I'd reunited with him when he'd been scared this morning had added weight to his trust in me. We raced up and down twice and he had to gamble on my not strangling him. It got rid of some energy and he was soon puffed. He's not fit. Another little breakthrough.

A little later the same day, and still with some light in the sky, a female friend who has volunteered in a dog sanctuary, entered the patio and then stood still, waiting over by the gate with the gate closed behind her, knowing that it's best to let a nervy dog decide for itself how it wants to react to the presence of an unknown human. Ursu ran out of the office to greet her - a love affair at first sight. Ursu knew instinctively that this was a good guy. It helped her being female and my obviously knowing her. Dog catchers in Romania, which he'd probably managed to dodge a few times before his luck ran out, are male.

We undertook a little test in the evening and left some cheese savouries in the office with Ursu whilst left on his own and he didn't take them. Perplexing really, given what a scavenger he's been all his life and how he squeals with delight when he hears his food going into his bowl. Maybe he's starting to recognise what's ours and what's his, and he doesn't pinch his leaders' food.

Day 29: 8th February

Ursu clocked my car coming down the drive whilst on the patio on his own just the day after his fearful outburst. He's known my car for a while and this was the first time he was on his own with me approaching in this way. My husband was in the kitchen and so maybe he felt secure on the patio on his own knowing someone was in the house behind him whereas yesterday he would have regarded us as retreating away from him. On immediate sight of my car, or maybe recognition of its motor sound from 200 yards away, Ursu became beside himself with exhilaration and started racing around and barking and jumping up and down with glee and throwing himself at the fencing. I'd been away from the house for about three hours. I took him into the office where he promptly had what we call a mad half hour - literally charging around and throwing his toys in the air. The dog experts say a dog mentally re-homes itself after four to five weeks. Maybe today marked the day.

Bolstered by his continuing development I ran him up and down the side lawn again and he then settled down between my husband and me on the lawn. He's now very relaxed having his lead put on but doesn't associate it with going for a walk. Why would he? He hasn't been off the plot to go for a walk and hardly knows what walking for pleasure means. The sooner he can witness other dogs doing it, the better will be his understanding.

Day 31: 10th February

I'd been out most of the day so my husband handled Ursu's outdoor training. Towards the end of the session Ursu slipped his collar and my husband quickly spurred him on back into the house. In the office in the evening I requested Ursu to come to me to put the collar back on, fully expecting him, after the two day pantomime of getting a collar on him around his 11th day with us, to be totally uncooperative. To my amazement he not only came up to me as requested but sat calmly whilst I put it back on (a little tighter this time) and without the lure of a treat. He did it simply because I'd asked him to. Magic. Although I later came to realise that he will often do something once just to let me know he understands the request and then resolutely refuse to do it again.

Ever since he arrived we've been trying to cultivate sociable table manners in a street dog whose instinct is to snatch and gobble. Whilst still very much in the territory of gobbling - he can demolish a plate full of food within five seconds - nevertheless he's learning to wait for the 'yes' command before pouncing on his food. Today we got to four seconds – I'm artful enough to say the 'yes' word a split second before I know his salivating mouth is about to dive in. We both get to win.

Day 32: 11th February

Another little step forward – literally. On his lead Ursu walked with me the 40 yards to the garage to welcome my husband home.

Day 33: 12th February

A female friend and her partner brought their 12 year-old Golden Retriever to meet Ursu. He coped with the numbers and was instantly affectionate towards our guests. He's definitely better with females than males, apart from my husband who he likes. He was very interested in the female retriever – the first dog he's had a chance to interact with since joining us a month ago - but she didn't reciprocate and he was gentlemanly enough not to push it.

We both went out in the evening for the first time leaving him on his own – with the office light on – for three hours. Previously we had only left the house together for 10 minutes at a time, and then deliberately ignoring him for a little while on our return to show that coming and going was no big deal. It was the same routine of being left in a closed crate with water and he was as cool as a cucumber when we returned home, helped, I believe, from having entertained visitors earlier in the day. His day had required a bit of sleeping off. Four humans and a dog in his little domain simultaneously was a lot for him to get his head round and we deliberately timed his first evening on his own to be after a tiring day when he would most likely be glad to settle down for an uninterrupted snooze.

Ursu definitely gave the sense of being a gentleman around our Golden Retriever visitor although it was around this time that he stared to develop a regular 'lipstick', as we say in modern parlance. He'd been castrated and showed no sexual interest in any person or object and he certainly didn't try to do anything with it. In time, roughly a couple of months later, it ceased happening and the vet when asked about it further down the line put it down to agitation. Ursu was nervously excited about life and everything and it was just a physiological reaction. Make of that what you will....

Days 34 - 36: 13th - 15th February

Our 13 year-old grandson came over to stay for a couple of nights and we used this shift of dynamics to extend Ursu's boundaries to include the whole of the office, not just his barricaded-off section, plus the dining room off the office. For the first time after just over a month with us Ursu saw himself as being 'accepted' into the pack's territory. His reaction was to hang back waiting for a verbal invitation to investigate his wider terrain. We saw this as no bad thing. By confining him to his personal territory for a month and a half he'd developed some self-confidence and a coping mentality, together with an acknowledgment of his status within the home.

Our grandson was understandably a little nervous of Ursu – not your average docile hound – but a good age of youngster to first introduce to a dog like this. Young enough to be considered a minor, old enough not to do anything rash with Ursu that would set things back. In taking on Ursu my husband and I had agreed that it was imperative that the dog could be trusted to be around children if he was to live with us permanently. As it was, we needn't have worried. A child had seemingly never done Ursu any wrong so Ursu didn't have an in-built problem with our grandson. By the second day the two of them had bonded and I was further relieved that my notion that Ursu was only the way he was because of the brutality he'd been subjected to and not because he was an inherently bad dog was boosted still further.

Ursu was starting to come out of his shell but in some ways this is when our work became harder. His instinct to seek freedom after years of being cooped up was extraordinarily strong. For those of you with naturally domiciled dogs it's probably hard to imagine the nanosecond it would take for Ursu to flee. He could move with the speed of a cheetah when he put his mind to it. We played table tennis with our grandson the first afternoon in our garage and took Ursu with us on the lead. The first thing he did was pee inside the door – clearly this was considered outside territory to him and not of his *own domain. We said 'no' after it was too late and he hasn't done it again since. But what he did do was bolt the second someone hit the electric door fob by mistake. He literally shot through the tiniest of gaps at the bottom and dashed into the wooded area across the drive. Luckily he became transfixed by the outdoors smells and we were able to get to him and slip his lead on whilst he remained distracted in the undergrowth.*

Indoors with less sensory distractions I can now get Ursu to 'stay' for five seconds from a stand of 20 steps back – still on the lead. And then he's had enough and does his own thing. Doubt we'd reach even five seconds outdoors where there are far better things to do.

Day 37: 16th February

Oh dear heavens. Today was scary. Ursu is naturally terrified of the vacuum cleaner and I obviously don't want him to associate me with something that panics him. So I ushered him onto his patio whilst I cleaned the office. I glanced out of the window a couple of minutes later and Ursu was out of his enclosure and nonchalantly meandering across the lawn sniffing. I was the one suddenly panicked but knew I couldn't call him or run up to him or he would dart. So I skimmed across the ground at break neck speed in a circle outside of his eye-line and then crept up behind him when he was two thirds down the drive and about to venture onto the main road. We live in a village but the road through, whilst not fast traffic, is constant enough and speedy enough to be a risk to both dog and vehicles. Luckily he was smelling the air. The smell of fresh air is truly novel to him and he will visibly inhale it in an almost trance-like state, holding his head up with his eyes closed, as might a human in their appreciation of a pleasant aroma. This gave me just enough seconds to clip his lead on before he'd registered what it was I was doing. But he then made it clear he wasn't prepared to walk. He simply stood stock still and wouldn't be encouraged to budge. So I picked up his 17 kilos and, like my husband some days earlier, carried him back to his patio, making sure a heavy stone was lodged against the gate which he had cunningly manoeuvred open in under three minutes. Bright dog.

Again, as with the experience with my husband, although entrapped, Ursu didn't show any signs of resistance but sat calmly in my arms. Whether, with his feet off the ground his survival instincts told him not to struggle, I don't know. And why he wouldn't come back to the house with me on his own four feet I don't know. Headstrong I guess. Perhaps he just wanted to stay outside and explore. But maybe the whole incident was a confusing mix of intrigue, confusion and burgeoning trust. I had never had such strong physical contact with him before and it was another little positive move forward.

Back in the office he went bonkers over a fly, jumping onto the windowsill and over his crate and all over the furniture trying to get at it – a massive unwarranted physical gymnastic display disproportionate to the event. He eventually, after much telling, responded to my commands to stop.

We keep a plastic water bottle next to his water bowl for topping up during the day. The plastic popped suddenly on some internal movement of air and he shifted swiftly from his day bed into the safety of his crate. It popped again and he came and sat next to me at my desk. Two signs in one day that he's starting to regard me as his protector.

Later in the afternoon, moving freely within his meshed secure garden, he started to cry with fright when a large van drove down the side driveway past him.

Days 38 - 42: 17th - 21st February

Ursu has only been with us six weeks and he continues to get better and better. I'm so proud of him. He trotted happily on his lead with me around the whole garden beyond his boundary fencing today and let me tug him gently in the right direction. He now wants to do his toilet in the larger garden beyond his fenced domain.

We've decided that Ursu has mastered enough of the basics to progress to being socialised around food more generally. For a dog that's had to scavenge and fend off starvation until the most recent year of his life when he was being sponsored by Monica and living in one of Romania's better kill shelters, it's remarkable that he lets us lift his bowl of food up when he's eating. We've done this only a couple of times to test his reaction, keen as we are for him to develop into being able to mingle without aggression within the wider world. You hear of otherwise gentle dogs flipping if anyone gets too close to them during mealtimes. It would be unreasonable to do this regularly and for any reason other than to gauge his temperament. We had wondered whether his facial scar suggested he would become a hostile fighting dog at mealtimes but we needn't have worried.

And none of us would like our plate of food taken away from us halfway through consumption – it's a form of provocation. Although thankfully not over-possessive with food, Ursu

does still become quite demented and almost frantic about nourishment. Not surprising given his background. He literally squeals with excitement when he so much as recognises the sound of his kibble being shaken into his food bowl from as far away as the kitchen. He then proceeds to run around in tight circles, breaking away to jump up like a rearing pony and jumping up and down over the office sofas. Witnessing the speed with which he can demolish a healthy portion of food really does have to be seen to be believed. He will also dive into soil and eat it – a sign, we're told, of malnourishment and missing nutrients. Grass has him salivating. Not because he feels sick but because he adores the moisture.

As I've mentioned, we have a formal dining room off the office which houses a six foot long dining table but my husband and I routinely eat in the kitchen at the other end of the house. Now, in our next stage of training him, looking like Lord and Lady Muck, we have been setting ourselves up each end of the long table to eat our dinner. We've done this three or four evenings making sure we've first fed Ursu so that the experience hasn't been too torturous for him and so that we ensure the best odds for a successful outcome. Whilst we've been eating he's been left to roam around the full office and dining room, and has been allowed to settle near us as long as he makes no dart for the food, which he hasn't. This evening we had cooked chicken – a regular dog's favourite – and upped the test by momentarily, for about two minutes, leaving the remains of our food in the room unattended before clearing away. He surpassed himself and didn't jump up to pinch any tasty nibbles. We then left the dining room door open onto the hallway. This has the front door there too but Ursu has only ever entered the home through the office doors directly into his personal home space. With the dining room door open he sits in the doorway and doesn't venture further into the hallway but is itching to do so. So that's good. He's curious and building in confidence but taking his cue from his pack leaders and not assuming he can run riot through the whole house which isn't yet his personal space.

One of the reasons for doing this, referencing back to the garage when he peed the moment he entered it, is that a dog won't willingly soil on its own territory. For Ursu to recognise wider boundaries beyond anything he could ever have experienced in the past, it was logical that we widened his world gradually. Once a dog starts defecating here there and everywhere, how do you reverse that? There's no way Ursu would have established a roomy Georgian house as his own territory on day one. The size of it alone would have terrified him, not knowing where to settle or what to do in the cavernous unsafe space. Through fear and lack of demarcation Ursu would have soiled in the house and, more importantly, been unhappy. By letting him build his confidence in restricted areas with just a couple of people around for the most part *and only venturing further on invitation, Ursu has progressed at a comfortable pace and healthy curiosity with no serious setbacks. For a dog that arrived carrying so much angst and fear, trying to go too fast with him over anything could have put an end to us ever managing to move him forward again.*

Day 43: 22nd Feburary

So much for yesterday's smugness that we are doing things right by Ursu. This morning he pooed for the first time ever in the house – in the dining room – and also did a pee in the same room. All I can suppose is that it was my fault. I didn't see him at all yesterday evening as, for the first time since he came to live with us, he was already settled for the night when I got in. Consequently he was especially excited when he first saw me this morning. Excitement in Ursu – having had nothing to be excited about for about seven years – quickly spirals into nervousness as his management of his emotions isn't yet balanced. I guess he's still not taking it for granted that this is his home. On this first evening when I didn't settle him for the night it's been enough to derail his confidence. He raced around in circles on greeting me this morning and after I'd gone back upstairs to shower the toilet accident occurred. A bit of a disappointment but no big deal. Dogs aren't robots. Things can go backwards for a dog that doesn't recognise the feeling of a guaranteed existence. My note to self is that when Ursu gets too excited – and I perhaps should have anticipated it – pull in the boundaries and re-boot.   I just tidied up and made no reference to it as far as Ursu was concerned. I know of someone who trained their dog not to soil in the house by vigorously rubbing their dog's nose in the mess. Very proud they were that their dog never did it again. Well, no, probably not.   But not a way to inspire trust and love, I would think. Ursu wouldn't have soiled if I'd managed things differently. The setback wasn't his fault.

Later in the day Ursu reacted peacefully to a dove in his house. My husband had saved one of our white doves from the clutches of a Sparrow Hawk, but not before the bird of prey had ripped its chest feathers out and lunched on its chest leaving a bloody cavity on show.   As I nursed it whilst my husband erected a temporary home for it indoors Ursu looked on without reacting or attempting to despatch a wounded bird, which would be a natural animal instinct. Ursu is going to be a sweet dog I'm sure. The dove lived by the way, living in harmony in a cage alongside Ursu until we were able to release it after six weeks with a miraculously fully-healed chest and sporting fresh feathers.

Day 44: 23rd February

Ursu raced up and down his enclosed side garden of his own volition today, on his own and off lead. It was a sheer joy to watch – a dog running around for the first time in its life from pure enjoyment rather than sheer panic. A very special moment. And a reminder to us as to how fast this dog can move. His speed of flight has surely kept him alive where others have perished.

With improved weather and the passage of time, now at nearly seven weeks with us Ursu is starting to regularly enjoy spending time unsupervised in his fenced patio and garden, taking in the air, trotting around and sniffing and just generally relaxing on the lawn. In the early days with us, his previous existence had been so limited that he was spooked by just about any moving sight as well as unfamiliar sounds and smells. Today he is taking in the birdlife, squirrels and rabbits with fascination.

He hasn't attempted to jump onto the sofa for days and days now and we've decided to let him sit on the outside bench if the fancy takes him, which he does when the ground is wet.

Day 49: 28th February

Today would have been Daisy's 18th birthday and what a fitting date to say we are now confident that Ursu is going to live happily with us from here on in for the rest of his life. Not to worry that unlike Daisy we shall never know Ursu's true age. It's enough that he's with us, saved, safe and ready to take on the life he's been missing all these years.

On what felt like a commemorative day, for the first time ever I walked him beyond our house on his lead to the big world outside – well, our local village anyway. We ventured out for about five minutes and at a quieter time of day. He came into contact with vans, other people and other dogs. He flinched at the passing vehicles, but dogs are great observers and as a fellow hound he witnessed other canines seemingly unperturbed at being walked around tied to a human by a long rope. He was watching and learning.

I introduced him to the car, opening the front door and encouraging him to jump into the back. I've a two door coupe. Needless to say he was on his lead. He'd only ever been in a crate in a car a couple of times and didn't understand what was being asked of him. After a few minutes he caught on, jumped onto the back seat and then proceeded to try and jump into the front to join me. Luckily I hadn't started the car up. I was just trying to begin the familiarisation. He may have found things a bit confusing, but there was no doubt that he was wallowing in the stimulation after years of complete nothingness other than fear.

But he did have an upset stomach in the night. We suspect he ate something bad in the garden. His instincts are in over-drive taking in everything and every sensory experience. Uncomfortably, he'd had to stay sat with his excrement in his closed cage overnight, sitting as far away from it as was physically possible. But I simply let him out and cleaned it all up, no words required.

Day 50: 29th February

Left on his own in the dining room for a few minutes, he did a small pee on the carpet. I think he was thrown by my husband's shouting from the lounge across the hallway during a Liverpool v Manchester City football match. Things can be tense in our household where Liverpool is concerned. Little reminders all the time that Ursu can become anxious or over-excited when things aren't totally calm around him.

At two months - a normal(ish) dog!

Ursu has been with us two months now and is pretty much a regular dog, so long as he's in our company for his confidence and also if we stick to a simple daily routine. Anything 'odd' and he's instantly nervy. When I say 'regular', I mean he's becoming reliable enough at the very basic level of dog socialisation to contemplate introducing him to a wider world. We never thought we would get this far with him ever, let alone so soon. A real cause for celebration. He's on the lead at all times and we can never afford to take our eyes off of him for a second when out and about. He's frightened of people and moving objects and traffic and is spooked very easily without warning.

At this juncture we only walk short distances together. I keep him on a short lead and walk him fast and close to me so he gets the message he's with me and this is what we do. I keep him on the inside of the pavement furthest from the traffic and by keeping him moving he's got less time to worry about his surroundings. I want to embed in him that he and I form a pack and that where I go he goes. He's not a free agent, back to roaming the streets on his own. One of the reasons we only walk for about five minutes is that he physically doesn't seem able to cope with more. He sits and refuses to budge further unless we turn back on ourselves homeward bound. I don't think his muscles have fully atrophied but he's certainly unfit and telling us as much.

We've popped him into the car and driven a couple of miles to some woods for a good romp, on an extendable lead. He absolutely adores the car with his head out of the window and the wind blowing through him. Such is his excitement that he actually tries to climb out of the window oblivious to the fact the vehicle is moving; all the while delivering a cacophony of frenetic sing-song. Presumably he thinks he can just hop back in when it suits him. He doesn't have much idea about life amongst humans. He also starts clambering to get out of a door or window the second the car stops, knowing what's coming next. Except he doesn't always know because sometimes we're at red lights. It's a game of chess manoeuvring ourselves out of the car whilst restraining Ursu from jumping over to the front seat and making a dash for it through any small gap. We have to be vigilant at all times.

He's still escaping from home now and again. With the best will in the world, opening the front door by a fraction and he can appear from nowhere and be gone. One day saw me with eyebrow dye on, and a hair colour on my head with a good two inch margin round my face to ensure full coverage, tearing down our back drive after him. Another evening my husband and I watched with incredulity as he pushed a three kilo stone away from his gate in 20 seconds flat and was off down the drive again. My husband has since reinforced the gate but even so, one split second after opening a door and this dog can appear out of thin air and be out through the crack before you can say 'oy'. On one occasion I threw the theory book out the window and screamed at him at the top of my voice to wait, just seconds before he was onto the main road. He was so startled he did just that, though I know better than to think the success of my frenzied outburst was anything other than one- off good luck.

On another occasion he got beyond the drive and returned home with a posse of villagers behind him, shooing him back down the drive. He'd refused to be befriended by them, or take a treat. Witnesses said he'd looked right and then left before crossing the road.

He's equally efficient at being elusive in the house. Frantically thinking he'd escaped yet again, we one day found him twenty minutes later huddled behind the dining room sofa in a tight ball. Oh how we laughed.

Walks can sometimes be a battle of wills. Diving onto a six-inch rancid chew one day, secreted along the roadside, saw me holding one end for a good two minutes telling him to drop it whilst he was trying to work the length into his mouth from the other side before he gave up in acknowledgement I'm the boss. I praised him enormously but he'd rather have had the chew.

He often gets his legs wrapped round the lead and my attempts to unravel him are acknowledged with a snap. I just carry on, defying him to hurt me, and he soon gets the message that it's an act of help.

We don't feel there's much to be gained by taking him to dog training classes - too much competing stimulation and no developed respect for humans.

In a nutshell - the first 8 weeks – getting to a baseline

- we hand-fed him through the security of his closed crate the first day

- we didn't react to his initial biting attempts the afternoon of his arrival

- I slept in the same room as Ursu for his first two nights as a reassuring quiet presence and without attempting to speak to him

- we strictly curtailed his boundaries to a small safe haven

- we replicated his Romanian shelter with a Ritz-style shelter that he could understand

- we didn't make eye contact or show our teeth and waited for him to come to us

- we spoke very gently.....just above a whisper

- we used very little vocabulary, i.e.

    - good boy
    - no
    - off
    - sit
    - stay
    - come here

- we ignored him a great deal whilst just being around him in a non-threatening way

- we never told him off but praised him when he reacted positively to a command

- we introduced him to the outside from the glass walled security of the indoors which he wasn't allowed to leave other than to go onto the patio area

- we lured him into his crate each night with a treat and closed the crate door for everyone's peace of mind

- we placed his crate next to the patio door so he instinctively went outdoors to do his toilet

- we let no-one other than ourselves see him for the first two weeks so that he learned to bond with us

- the radio was put on low for him each morning so that human voices became non-threatening

- I allowed him to 'mouth' my hand for the first three weeks as a puppy does to bond with its Mum. Then like a Mum I began walking away when he did it, graduating to the 'no' word so he began to understand the significance of the word

- he was introduced to a lead first by leaving it on the floor next to a treat and graduating up from that. With regards his collar we donned thick gloves and got this on him on Day 11 through a joint effort of planned choreography, split-second timing and the bribery of treats

- we walked him on the lead up and down the patio and then our garden for weeks before taking him beyond our home boundaries

- we fed him dry food in small regular amounts and kept treats plain while we assessed his constitution and in order to keep his excitement under control.

At three months

By the third month we were venturing a little further into adjoining fields which we can reach on foot from our house within five minutes. We live in a very hilly area and Ursu would pull to get to the top of a ridge where he'd promptly sit down and do a 360 degree survey of the landscape – no doubt checking out for danger and approaching dog catchers. He still has a preference for high ground where he can't be taken by surprise by any approaching threat. He'd also in the early days got an inbuilt urge to run for exit points. No matter how large the field was that he was in, he'd scout round for sight of a gated fence and make a bee line for it, as best he could on an extendable lead. Once in such a field his lead broke and he disappeared within a flash. He's got that same flabbergasting talent that five tonne elephants have for becoming invisible in the bush in one clean movement. Knowing his penchant for making a break for it I didn't know what to do. Would he run through the gate onto the main road and become involved in a collision? Might he run home – he was certainly smart enough to work out his bearings. Or might his street dog DNA kick in and we never see him again? He wouldn't have allowed anyone to go anywhere near him, even with food. I had images of him becoming a professional stray again with enough savvy to get by through scavenging. I rang my husband who said he would ring me back if Ursu turned up home. This in itself would have meant crossing a main road used as a thoroughfare by busy traffic. My heart was in my mouth. Should I search the fields or stay put in the hope he would come back to me – something he had never done before? At best we could get him to come to us on the command of 'come here' and then only at home indoors with no other distractions to get the better of him. A full eight minutes passed whilst I called out to him without moving too far away from the spot where his lead had broken.

Then, just as quickly as he'd disappeared he flashed into view again, came right up to me and calmly sat down in front of me waiting for me to put his lead back on. This was incredible. Getting him to sit to have his lead put on before leaving the house was a regular battle. He would be too excited and impatient. I would regularly have to walk away from him and then try again until he got the message that he wasn't going to be allowed to run hell for leather out of the door simply because I'd picked his lead up. Yet here he was, in the big outdoors with all the wonder it had to offer, calmly inviting me to reattach his lead. It was as though he was trying to tell me that I could start to trust him a little bit more. Nice try, I thought Ursu, but you're going to have to demonstrate a little bit of consistency before we do this again. Eight minutes is way too long to be absent without leave. But I praised him for coming back to me. He would have regarded a scold as a disincentive to return to me another time.

On each of our returns from walks I would enter the office first and he would come in after me on invitation, something he still does to this day.

Ursu is clearly becoming bored and keen to break out and test his wits within the neighbourhood. So around this time we decided to take our life in our hands and walk to a pub and sit outside with him. It's strange looking back that we would be feeling so tentative about what other people take for granted in terms of enjoying time with their pets. But this was no ordinary dog. He arrived frightened of everybody and everything and rather than cower he would flee or defend. We were anxious to avoid a scene and so we first made sure he'd been walked off his feet, which in his unfit state was about 30 minutes, to increase the chances of his wanting to settle. We sat outside the pub. We kept him on a very short rein and asked him to sit. He did. We gave him water. We made sure either one of us was between him and people coming and going. Some people even stopped to admire him – he's a cute dog and still mistaken for female – but we didn't encourage interaction. Heaven knows what mayhem would have erupted had anyone tried to touch him. We stayed about half-an-hour and quit whilst we were ahead. We didn't give him a treat as we just wanted 'calm'. Boy, were we buoyed up. It felt like a real breakthrough moment and we were so proud of him.

I mentioned earlier that Ursu was developing a slightly protective streak. Barking at the postman – something he had earlier dropped – had re-entered his repertoire. This was our fault because of the configuration of his 'home' overlooking the driveway.   His barking always resulted in the postman retreating after delivering the mail, so in Ursu's mind his barking was proving effective.   His wish was the postman's command. In his mind the postman left because Ursu had told him to. If we stood in front of Ursu and occupied his space he'd stop barking. If we're not with him then he's his own boss.

As we opened up the house to him in months two and three we introduced him from the dining room across the hallway through to the lounge. He was only allowed a few feet up the hallway and not into the kitchen. He understood this invisible boundary and by and large respected it.   What would make him break rank was the noise of a popping cork from a bottle of Prosecco. It was just too much and he would let out a bark. But rather than retreat from the scary unknown, this dog, who, when we got him couldn't cope with noise above the sound of a whisper, would run towards the un-established danger onto the front line. He'd come running up to the kitchen door and check that I was OK. "Prosecco is always OK", I would tell him. He wouldn't cross the line into the kitchen and would then allow me to guide him back to the invisible boundary.   Small signs that I mattered to him.

Other than my husband catching up with the horseracing with Ursu on our smallish office TV screen positioned on the wall, Ursu hadn't been introduced to the entertainments world. The most he'd experienced was dulcet tones on the radio. We've a 42 inch screen TV at floor level on a table in the lounge and we first introduced Ursu to the tele one evening with the whole thing switched off. The next day we had the picture on but the sound off. The third evening we had both picture and sound, but at low volume. I think it's very impressive that a street dog like this could very quickly process the TV for what it is – a set of inanimate objects, be they images and sounds of animals or humans. He would look up at the screen now and again and cock his ear at the sounds of a canine, but there was never the suggestion that he thought it was something for real that required investigation.

There was just one time when he suddenly fled the lounge in panic. It had been an X Factor staging that did it. But then the X Factor can be enough to rattle the nerves of the best of us. The backdrop became a flash of lights like fire and there must have been a connection in his mind of something fearful he had endured in his past. We turned the TV over, not off, and invited him back in before the fear took root and he chose to come back to us. To this day he's not fond of our outdoor chimenea or indoor open fire. I've read that as well as the other barbaric ways of disposing of dogs in Romania, they are also hanged and burned alive on pyres, at least in Ursu's time there, and he will most likely have witnessed this.

Each evening I would sit on the floor of the lounge with him, attempting deeper bonding. This wasn't the sweet picture one might imagine, as Ursu was still unhappy having parts of his body touched other than the top of his head and the top of his back. Ursu was particularly snappy about his paws. A dog's paws are naturally sensitive and his had never been touched before. If I so much as dared put a finger on one of them he'd snap at me, though he didn't feel the need to growl as well. It was important that Ursu came to let me nearer to him if I was to be able to check him over for general health. I mentioned earlier how he'd sit for hours and chew his nails. Although not short they'd naturally become worn down over time with us with no pain to Ursu, and other than his nightly grooming he'd lost interest in his constant chewing of them. But I needed to be able to feel for lumps and bumps too.

I've referred earlier to the subject of a snappy dog and our natural reaction to flinch and step back. But I couldn't let this dog think that he was in charge. Much to my husband's disapproval of my tactic, when Ursu snapped I would touch his leg and paw again, ignore his protest and stroke his head lightly and extremely briefly. I'd then leave it and do the same the next night and the next. My husband felt I was building up a problem with the dog but the reverse happened. Over a period of time, and it did take patience, Ursu gave up the fight and today, two and a bit years on, Ursu can't get enough bodily contact with me and there is no part of his anatomy that is out of bounds, though I don't fancy risking my chances in trimming his nails. Touching his front paws offended him less than it did his back ones so I'd focus on the front ones and make irregular contact with the back ones. It took four months of this before his recalcitrant behaviour stopped. And I only attempted it in the evenings when he had a full tummy and was at his most acquiescent. His snaps were a warning shot and I took a gamble that, two months in, his bond with me had grown to such a point that he wouldn't want to bite me. Just as an aside he'd extended his bedtime from 6.00pm to about 8.00pm by this time and now he likes to be tucked up by 10.00pm, but can cope with later.

Walking him one day someone asked me his name. Thinking I'd temporarily had a lapse of memory before recalling his identity as 'er....Su', I was challenged as to why I'd called a male dog by a female moniker. This made me question whether we were right to stick with the name Ursu, but I reminded myself that we liked the name. In any event kids loved it. The weirder the sound the better as far as a child is concerned and, unlike adults who need to hear a wacky word several times before learning it, children catch on to the name Ursu instantly. And then there are those people who connect the name with the Planets Ursa Major and Minor. Ursu will still answer to Nelson for the few who prefer the name even when he's not heard it for months. The downside of his second name is the irony of his facial scar – which we weren't aware of until he joined us – and its connection with Horatio Nelson. I find myself doing all the explanations I'd hoped to avoid by renaming him. I don't think we'll consider a third name. Ursu is just fine and he looks pretty anyway.

One day when out walking him two young toddlers touched his head without warning. He sat and just let it happen. Young children had never hurt him so he didn't have an issue.

The Vets: The vets in Romania had terrified Ursu. Being castrated without anaesthetic must have been a dreadful experience. So a friend suggested I desensitise Ursu by simply taking him to our local vets and sitting in reception a few times before he needed any actual veterinary attention. Ursu happily trotted in, sat calmly and seemed unfazed, and we repeated this three or four times over a period of weeks. On one of the visits I asked a vet passing through reception to estimate his age. "No older than seven" he opined, though his dark teeth suggested greater seniority and the vet didn't get too close. When I asked whether I should muzzle him for his first appointment the vet replied, "Does he look like a dog that needs to be muzzled to you?" I agreed not. How wrong we both were.

During this period I tied him on his lead outside the library for less than a minute as a test. Ursu was calm in this quiet environment, but the exercise of securing the lead had to be done without my holding Ursu's collar and in the split of a second before he darted.

On one occasion, blinded by lashing rain, I didn't secure his lead properly to the bars outside the village mini-supermarket. We were still at the stage where I couldn't risk releasing my grip of him during the manoeuvre or he'd be off like lightning and he still wasn't overly fond of me touching the scruff of his neck. It made the whole operation pretty tricky. A couple of minutes later, and now inside the shop, I sensed something behind me. Sure enough, when I turned around, there he was nonchalantly ambling down the aisle behind me having negotiated the shop's sliding doors to enter.

I introduced Ursu to water at the local reservoir in his third month, but he showed no interest despite being treated to a visual display of what fun can be had by throwing one's body into the water to retrieve a stick. But he is watching and observing other dogs and working out for himself that being tied to a human is a good and happy thing, bizarre as it must seem to him.

Taking a tip from another friend, we have replaced the usual dental sticks which Ursu devours in one second flat with carrots. They are cleaning his teeth up nicely. For a dog that spent years starving and then existing on dry kibble, Ursu loves the crunchy moisture of not just carrots but also raw celery, cucumber and peppers, in fact any raw vegetable not harmful to dogs, which onions for example are. He also enjoys apples, pears (minus the toxic pips) and screams excitedly at the mere sight of them.

We have various visitors to the house, including young children, and Ursu is friendly towards them all, though he'll only let young children stroke him. That's good enough for us at this stage and is particularly important.

In my efforts to minimise Ursu's 'Scarlet Pimpernel' antics I've created some posters placed strategically around the house asking the kids to come and get a pass from me to be able to enter a room I know Ursu to be in. Posters are also on all exit points. Generally the kids get the message better than the adults do.

With a penchant to slither rather than jump Ursu managed to creep through this opening

Four months

I left Ursu for a couple of hours with one of our dog lover friends who he'd accepted in his own home and his school report was that he'd been a 'gentleman'. This soon led to us being able to leave him with the friend overnight. Ursu was beyond excited to be reunited with me, crying and racing around like a demented pet on speed, but it was clear he'd been happy whilst there and has contentedly gone back since. As time progresses he's still over the moon to see us again but the high-pitched 'I can't believe it' squealing has abated.

Now when male visitors come to the house we ask them to quickly snap Ursu's lead on and off in our efforts to gradually wean him off his fear of men. By and large Ursu co-operates in a slightly impatient, would rather it wasn't happening, kind of way. But there's no aggressive reaction.

Five months

Five months on and there is still absolutely no way we can risk letting Ursu off a lead. In fact he was with us nine months before we were even remotely confident enough to give this a go. But at five months he started to mellow when walking past trucks and floating bin bags and leaves and other startling detritus. I began teaching him 'go home', letting him off his lead just feet away from the patio gate. I only dared do this when I was sure he'd built up enough of a thirst to want to head straight for his water on his patio.

Ursu has started to moult. So hairy is he that losing hair is a constant occurrence. But this is on another scale. I'd earlier cut across his matted tail in one swift movement whilst he was distracted by his meal and it was growing back. We thought we understood thick coats having had a retriever but Ursu would shed a supermarket bag full (uncompressed) every day. As well as it dropping out in lumps, I would run my hands through his coat – no chance at this time of introducing a brush. This went on every day for six weeks. We then had a month off and the same thing began again for another six weeks. It was as though his improved diet had caused a complete regeneration of his coat. Underneath was new lighter, silky soft hair that feels like velvet to this day and attracts lots of compliments and I'm sure Ursu feels more comfortable for it. And he looks half the width. But his coat did its job when he needed it most and helped save him.

Ursu's very heavy coat before the big moult

Ursu is friendly towards other dogs despite having been in competition with them for his survival although he does freak out when he sees a Husky – possibly the breed that he had an altercation with and bears the scar of. Or it could simply be a fear of the piercing eyes of the husky. He's certainly not afraid of my eyes and after our initial introduction when I deliberately avoided eye contact with him he's gone on to favour gazing into my eyes, quite softly and without dominance. As he's developed in confidence I've introduced noise into our play so that he forgets the association of noise with fear. I also put my hand over his eyes from time to time, just briefly, to build up trust in me – nothing bad ever happens no matter what I do with him.

Six months

A Boat Trip: The most incredible thing to-date. Ursu came on a three day boat trip with us, just the three of us. I put him in a life jacket and was surprised he let me and which attracted several quips from observers about my not knowing adult dogs could naturally swim. Swim he might be able to but we weren't sure how he would react and whether we would need to sweep him out of the water before he disappeared under the boat's propeller if he misjudged his novel surroundings. His behaviour was that of an excitable puppy experiencing and learning things for the first time, as indeed he was. As it happens, he had a couple of dodgy moments on the canal's bank when he judged green to represent terra firma when in actuality it was often straggly grass over water. But I watched him the whole time, and kept him on his lead of course, and soon raked him backwards onto firm ground and he was quick to analyse and pick up what was what. He loved the boat and was as cool as a cucumber as he sat on the deck whilst we went over a viaduct scores of metres above the ground.

Biting through his lead: With family over for the weekend we took Ursu into the garden to be with us and tied him to one of the chairs. He was perfectly happy until we moved away just a few feet from him, although still very much in view. He promptly bit through his lead and headed back to the house. At least he made for the right direction.

Eight months

Rosette: Monica's Romanian Rescue held its annual fundraising in Yorkshire and Ursu made his debut appearance. He was frightened by the tannoy system and did a pee against a white stone in his nervousness - except it wasn't a stone but the T shirt being worn by a friend sat on the ground. She was sanguine about it. He wasn't comfortable or relaxed and pulled like mad on his lead but this led to extra vigour in the ring where he won best senior dog. What a star.

Trip to France: Buoyed by Ursu's ability to get his head round new situations quickly as long as he is with one of us, we decided to take him with us on a fortnight's trip to France, which included a three night stay in a hamlet with family. This required quite a bit of thinking through and anticipation. The eve of our Eurotunnel crossing we stayed in a hotel down south. The road was busy, the hotel had other guests and Ursu was completely spooked - a lot of barking and straining went on and he would have darted to who knows where had I not hung on to his lead for grim death the whole time. In the Eurotunnel, safe in the vehicle he knew, and with us with him, he coped with the strangeness of the journey and its noises. The first French hotel we stopped at he wasn't at all sure about entering via a revolving door. But then spectacularly he'd already recovered from the scary concept of sharing his accommodation with others just the night before and took in his stride the comings and goings of other visitors. One thing Ursu had taught us early on was that he never barked whilst in the car, something we were extremely grateful for. And yet, one morning driving away from a French overnight hotel where Ursu had behaved impeccably (always on the lead of course), he went into a frenzy when he spied a French post woman on her bike with a lattice basket at the front. Why? We have no idea. He had never barked at anything or anybody from the car before and he hasn't done so since and yet for some reason known only to him this innocuous sight triggered some fearful memory.

As we travelled down through France we stayed in a budget hotel teeming with people where he sat docilely by us in the restaurant amidst all the comings and goings and aroma of food. Unbeknown to us a dog behaviourist – one of a group of bikers - was watching him and later congratulated us on Ursu's excellent behaviour. He was staggered when he learnt the back story of only eight months previous and another biker credited it to having a raised bone on the back of the head. It is a sign of canine intelligence according to his family who were dog breeders. Whether this is true or not we don't know but Ursu is certainly a dog that picks things up in a trice. I mentioned the post woman and bike incident and Ursu's extraordinary reaction. The dog behaviourist said that we have no idea the full extent of what Ursu has witnessed and experienced in the seven or so years before he came to us and it is as simple as that. For Ursu there was a mental connection between a seemingly charming gentle country scene and something terrible. We would never know what it was.

Pride comes before a fall. Wallowing in the compliments bestowed upon us and our evidently inherent knowledge of how to handle a stressed dog, the very next night and in clear view of the proprietor of another restaurant Ursu jumped up, plonked both front paws on the tablecloth and nicked a piece of bread off the table in a room in which we were the only guests. We were mortified and apologetic and came to realise that where bread and Ursu are concerned discipline goes out of the window. He doesn't care whether it's fresh or stale. And on that behavioural trait we're not bemused. Tossed bits of discarded lunch will have been his mainstay when surviving on the streets and his DNA was programmed to dive for it no matter his surroundings. He's the same with discarded serviettes. Luckily the French are very accepting of dogs, even in restaurants.

Whilst at the family hamlet, comprising of about eight properties with the nearest main road a couple of kilometres away, we dared for the first time to let Ursu off his lead to come and go as he pleased. Knowing he didn't have a geographical understanding of where he was we calculated on his sticking close. And what he chose to do was to undertake repeat circuits of the hamlet, checking in with us each time he'd finished a lap. We were over the moon, albeit a French family without the dog- loving gene didn't quite appreciate his repeated courtesy visits to them. Their son of about nine or ten years of age was enjoying riding his bike and Ursu took it upon himself to chase the lad, barking. We were apologetic but the deed was done. And there was that connection with bikes again. Puzzlingly Ursu isn't bothered about bikes in the UK – maybe because he's only encountered them on roads keeping to a straight line well away from his personal path.

Knowing he's not allowed upstairs at home but not wanting to be downstairs on his own in a strange house he would climb the stairs and sit outside the host's bedroom overnight. Smart.

Returning to England it's a requirement to have a vet's visit and to take worming tablets. Ursu went mad in the vets – screaming and thrashing about. With perfect paperwork the female vet took a pragmatic attitude and allowed me to administer the tablets. Ursu will digest anything he's given. Medication carries the same thrill as treats. Glucosamine, worming tablets – he'll take them straight from the hand and won't isolate them if added to his meal. It all goes down. Despite the vet being a gentle female and all the work I'd done introducing Ursu to a vet environment back home, it was another reminder of his past that spiralled him into 'the mist'.

We made a late decision to return home three days earlier than originally planned. Paperwork at the ferry crossing has to be spot on to the finest degree. Although Ursu's vaccinations were up-to-date and evidently so, the UK vet stamp hadn't been recorded as minutely accurately as required. Ursu got back into England on his Romanian stamps that were due to expire three days later. Luck was on his side once again.

He was overjoyed to get back home and apart from the vet visit the whole trip had been pretty much a success. We thought to ourselves that we might make taking him away with us a regular thing, as indeed we did. The next venture was Spain.

Nine months

Off the lead: At nine months we decided to take the plunge and test Ursu off his lead. We took him to a wide open field with no escape routes onto the main road. In hindsight we'd wished we'd videoed him, but as with his aggressive behaviour, his extremes of reactions aren't captured for the basic reason that it's always been a case of all hands to the deck, often with our hearts in our mouths apprehensive as to what might happen. My husband detached his lead and we watched. What he did was to career round and round in sheer and abandoned joy in large circles the size of a horse dressage arena. This went on for three minutes or so at break neck speed with his body angled low to the ground like a biker dicing with balance looking like he might topple over at any second onto his side. He then came literally galloping back to us, skidded towards us along the grass and threw himself at our feet looking up at us with sheer happiness. Another truly special moment. His evident happiness has since been remarked upon by fellow walkers observing that he almost smiles as he trots about.

And so began the long haul of recall training. The day his lead had snapped in the field and he'd reappeared after eight minutes of doing his own thing, calmly inviting me to reattach his lead, had evidently been Ursu doing no more than training me to comprehend that he understands exactly what I want of him, and not that he's willing to docilely oblige each time. I can be within a hair's breadth of attaching his lead and he will twist and dart and run away whilst I am ineffectively reinforcing commands to 'stay'.

I introduced him to a whistle the day after he was treated to a demonstration of its use by a fellow dog walker and his hound. Ursu had only watched the dog's recall twice but he instantly got it. The next day, armed with treats, I blew the whistle and asked Ursu to come to me. He did. I did the same thing again, but without the verbal accompaniment and he repeated it receiving a treat again. And then he stopped, once more informing me that 'Ok I'll let you know I understand what you're on about but I'm not really interested in doing it again as there's nothing in it for me'. Because when outdoors, treats have no allure for Ursu. After years of being cooped up, there is nothing in the world as enticing as the love of the moment in the great outdoors with its smells and experiences and the chance to run for joy and eat grass and soil. Getting Ursu to do recall has been a slow process and he's still apt to do his own thing when the sensory overload is too much for him and everything becomes a blur with voice instructions screened out, sometimes deliberately and at other times quite innocently. We never let him off the lead until we know the circumstances bode well. Eighty per cent of each of his daily walks is now off lead. It has taken nerves of steel to not follow him but stay rooted to the spot and demand that he return to us.

If he started to wander off and ignore the recall instruction we would carry on our path a few steps to visually tell him he either came with us or got left behind. As soon as we were sure he couldn't see us we'd hide behind a tree and watch him. When he sensed he'd lost us he'd start coming back at which point we would let ourselves become visible to him again, still with our backs turned to him, and carry on walking away from him as though we'd never loitered. As he caught up with us we'd praise him for returning. Our problem was that his burgeoning confidence and street-life mentality meant that if the coast looked otherwise clear – such as no-one around to catch him and whisk him away - he was just as happy to do his own thing and meet us back at home. More than once saw us abandon our hideaway and do a circuitous helter-skelter dash so that he couldn't see us, to then reappear in front of him with our backs to him gasping for breath. In this way he continued to walk towards us rather than us be seen to be chasing to catch up with him, again reinforcing that he followed us, not the other way around. And then we started taking him out in the car more regularly to unknown places that he couldn't navigate his way home from and very gradually, and only through consistent training supported by a growing bond, did his recall improve. Sometimes in my efforts to keep him unsure of his bearings I confused myself and on more than one occasion relied on Ursu to guide us back to the car.

One year

Taking a muzzle: At one year with us Ursu had become more and more like a pet dog. It's taken twelve months for him to relax fully to the point where he will roll completely onto his back exposing his underside. He's never exhibited strange habits to speak of, other than the nail biting which has ceased, and which he now rations to his nightly grooming regime. And so 16 months in, we travelled to Andalucia in Spain to dog-sit for family and took Ursu with us, driving through France and Spain following a short ferry crossing.

The ferry crossing required Ursu to wear a muzzle for embarkation and disembarkation and I was very anxious about this and irresponsibly left training until as late as possible, unconvinced that I was going to succeed with him. To my surprise it took just two weeks to get Ursu to accept a muzzle and I was overjoyed. I began by buying the most comfortable model and worth the extra few pounds. I would smear it with sandwich paste and leave it on the floor for him to lick. I progressed to holding the muzzle in my hand whilst he licked it. I then positioned the muzzle in such a way that he had to put his head in the muzzle for a split second to get the reward. I built up the time until I was able to loosely strap the muzzle on and then hand feed him even greater rewards. Able to eat

and drink through it, the muzzle didn't distress him but he would nevertheless try and shake it off as an unnecessary irritant. All of this was done indoors without external distractions. When it got to the point I could get the muzzle on but he would try and discard it, I started taking him for a very fast walk whilst wearing it and letting his surroundings become the distraction. We only progressed at the speed we did because of his developed trust in me.

The ferry crossing to France was short and Ursu remained in the car where he felt safe despite his strange surroundings and the unusual sounds. We reached Andalucia after four overnight stops and Ursu behaved impeccably at each of the hotels. As we got out of the car the family's two dogs, who we know well, came to greet us. Both campo (countryside) dogs, male and female, they are equally very large, the male weighing 44 kilos and nicknamed Head of Security for his serious guarding instincts. All seemed well so we brought Ursu out of the car on his lead and kept him close to us. Fireworks erupted minutes later when the host offered Ursu an existing old dog's bed and the male was livid. He literally pounced onto Ursu barking ferociously and kept him pinned to the floor until the host intervened. Ursu's intelligent response was to be submissive. He decided to play the long game and took himself off to the large car park area and sat under one of the vehicles for a couple of hours, waiting for the male to calm down. Distressing as the scene had been we all knew better than to make a big deal of it. Dogs sort their relationships out themselves and the male was very noisily telling Ursu who was boss and Ursu played by the house rules. We have subsequent footage of them playing together in the three weeks that Ursu shared their home but he always played second fiddle to the resident male and waited for the other dog to initiate friendship. Sparks would fly at mealtimes when the resident male was at his most unforgiving and we learned to keep them apart around food and also at night. But the two campo dogs had been so well trained that they wouldn't touch their food until given the go ahead by their owner who could go as far as to get into the car and start driving away before giving them the 'yes' word. The dogs would be transfixed on their owner for anywhere up to two or three minutes without attempting to sneak a morsel. There was a hilarious cameo moment early on when I had put food down for the two resident dogs thinking Ursu was safely out of the way. In his inimitable way Ursu appeared from nowhere and scrunching his 17 kilo build down as flat as possible, he stealthily sneaked along the ground like a snake in front of the two dogs and snatched some food from Head of Security's plate whilst his eyes were pinned on me waiting for the 'yes' command, all the while oblivious to the audacious theft. Another illustration of Ursu's cunning and his individual way of dealing with things that help explain how he survived his years in Romania.

Each morning I would start out with the three of them for walks together along the tracks around the Finca but invariably ended up as 'Billy No Mates' with Ursu, off lead, pathetically trying to keep up with the other two who would scale hillsides in seconds flat and disappear for minutes at a time. In the end I resorted to keeping Ursu on his lead for his own dignity and survival. And unlike the Spanish dogs who could take the 35 degree heat, despite Romania's hot summers Ursu was as floored by the temperature as I was and the morning exercise became done and dusted by 8.00am when Ursu would then seek shade for the remainder of the day.

But Ursu's intolerance of the beating heat came to nought when the greater need for affection reared its head.

He and the female dog had quickly become best buddies with both sharing a desire to be loved by humans but with the female better able to withstand the heat and therefore stick by me. One morning as I lay on the sunbed I felt Ursu gradually creep onto the bed inch by inch in slow motion and then slither along to lay first claim on me.

Returning home we drove as far as northern Spain and caught the ferry back to England. Ursu was as good as gold again when it came to putting his muzzle on at the port. I'd reintroduced it to him with the help of treats a couple of days before leaving Spain. The limited number of dog-friendly cabins was sold out and so we had no other option but to book him into the kennels on the top deck. Of all the dogs in their crates I would say Ursu was the most chilled. He took in his stride the regular but short visits I made to him during the day and his overnight stay in a single crate alongside the other hounds. Some owners spent the full visiting hours between 6.00 a.m. and 11.00 p.m. camped out on the cramped smelly portion of deck apportioned to their pets in a bid to calm them but Ursu was less demanding. A stoic dog and not afraid.

He loved his time in the car, which is just as well as we travelled over 2,500 miles there and back.

Just before leaving Spain we had a repeat pantomime at the vets where we'd taken Ursu for health clearance, only, unlike in France, this time he almost jumped through an open window one floor up as the vet attempted to put him on the consultation table. My husband and I grabbed hold of him just in time. Had he succeeded he would have plummeted down the rock face that was on the other side of the wall. Ursu's reaction had been so violent my husband was badly shaken. Ursu was back to his calm self again the moment we left the consulting room but it took a while longer for my husband to get his equilibrium back.

Two years and onwards

Ursu is a lovely dog and much admired when out and about. He has a beautiful fluffy soft-as-velvet coat and smells sweet despite never having been washed. His breath is fresh despite his poor teeth and he takes great pride in his personal grooming, something that would have been impossible for him for years on end in his previous life. Visitors are automatically offered a lint brush, as he is still the hairiest dog we've ever had. I vacuum almost daily. There is no part of his body now out of bounds to me and out on a walk he will proffer a paw if he's got a thorn stuck, though I will never attempt to clip his nails which thankfully he has got under control through his own efforts. He is my shadow and invariably under my feet and if I inadvertently catch his tail or a paw under my foot, he instantly forgives and isn't stressed.

His fascination with food never wanes and two plus years on he still runs round and round in circles in giddy anticipation. But he has managed to stop the squealing. He waits for the 'yes' word before diving into his food and says thank you after a meal by coming to look for me and giving me a lick - in fact he gives me a quick thank you lick in appreciation of anything I do to help him - but he never asks for his meals, even as a prompt when they're served up a little late.

Any food left anywhere below waist height he regards as fair game and will snatch it, unless he knows it to be the remnants of my husband's or my food in which case he leaves it untouched. I once inadvertently left a piece of cheese on a low coffee table in the office overnight and it was still there the following morning which I must admit astounded me. But at a special birthday party with the house full of guests he was caught snaffling all the pies from a low table.

His table manners have improved vastly and as I proffer a treat I say the word 'gentle' delivered 'sotto voce' and he straight away calculated that he mustn't snatch.

He's still pleased to see me in the mornings and greets me with me a grin (a sign of deference) and leans into me for affection but he's no longer overexcited or vocal which is a good thing. He's becoming more balanced. Neither does he still scream at the sight of scissors but there's no way he would tolerate a trip to a grooming salon and so when I need to trim his bum hair I add gravy to his meal which affords me an extra ten seconds to quickly snip. Before I happened upon this method I would take a pair of nail scissors with me on walks and whilst he was entertaining himself smelling the undergrowth I would manage a quick trim, all the while praying that a fellow walker wouldn't appear in the picture and think me crazy. He's grown to adore being brushed by me and would stand it all day but other than my husband and a family child, won't let others groom him.

His spatial awareness from the day he joined us has amazed us. Apart from an early occasion when he knocked over the barrier in his 'shelter' he's not had a single accident with a glass or ornament and despite his pom-pom tail and there usually being a bottle of wine around in the evenings.

Although he now enjoys a cushioned existence, when there is heavy rain outside, out of instinct he will retreat to his crate for protection, one of the few times he favours his crate these days daring now to lie out in the open. And on the coldest sub-zero nights he still opts to sleep in the office even though the warmer dining room is left open for him.

He has mastered a wide range of vocabulary and these days we can speak to him at a normal pitch. We mainly include hand movements with voice which will help him if, as with

Daisy, he goes on to lose his hearing. He's a well-balanced and obedient dog, though he does still possess the wandering urge of the street dog if left unattended. He's got an escape proof boundary in the garden - another of my husband's hand-made creations - and loves chilling out on his own, safe in his environment. If anyone ever tried to take him I vouch they would come off the worse in the inevitable hullaballoo.

Out together on a walk he responds to the 'wait' instruction and will listen for the 'yes' word before jumping over a stile, even off lead. And we can now open an exterior door confident that he will respect the command to stay and not run hell for leather down the drive.

His happiness at being outdoors is palpable and infectious. Accustomed as he's become to the comfort of being able to dry off after a trip out there's no weather that will deter him from his daily exercise and in the worst of conditions when there are no other dog walkers around and it's just Ursu and me it reminds me that the simple pleasures in life are often the best.

He's not had a day's illness in all the time we've had him and apart from the occasional upset stomach from too much sniffing around he's not required any medical treatment other than the obvious preventative procedures. Alas he is still traumatised by the vets despite our best efforts and likely

always will be given his experiences in Romania. He'll happily trot into a consultation room and accept a treat dispensed by the vet but the second they approach brandishing anything as innocuous as a microchip reader he starts flailing and squealing with fear. At last year's annual vaccinations he slipped his collar and muzzle in his 'Wall of Death' imitation notwithstanding the best efforts of a vet and three nurses. The vet in his kindness hadn't wanted Ursu to associate me with his fear of the environment and had opted to handle him without me present. Now we lightly sedate him to the point where he is slightly sleepy but still awake and walking, as one might a dog afraid of fireworks. It works as long as I stay with him and everything is done crouched on the floor well away from the consultation table. I feed him a treat (breadsticks of course) whilst the vet comes up behind him and injects him in the back rather than the usual spot in the scruff of the neck. Ursu is oblivious and I'm grateful to our vet for being willing to still see him despite the earlier scratched arms. It means the vet can also check his eyes and ears and general health, and has been able to verify his likely age. People have asked why I bother to voluntarily immunise Ursu when his immune system must be second to none having survived alongside disease and the dead but he's older now and I couldn't bear the thought of his now going down with something avoidable having withstood so much.

Once terrified of the vacuum cleaner, now when he hears it from another room he runs towards it knowing a human is on the other end.

He is so affectionate it's unbelievable. He's swung from shunning human contact to craving being stroked and love is the one thing he will demand. Food and walks and games he hopes for in pleasant anticipation and with immeasurable patience. But affection he asks for and has become the most tactile dog we've had. He likes nothing more than to burrow his head into me as if seeking protection and takes deep inhalations of my scent.

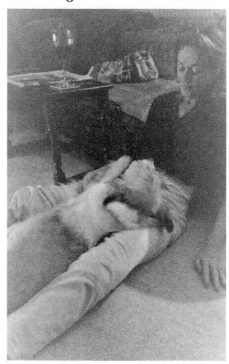

Ursu debunks one professional view that dogs don't like being touched and only tolerate it to appease their owner. Ursu has set his own rules on this one. And when he considers he's been given a decent level of affection he will lick as if to say "and now it's my turn to give."

He understands and respects the rules of the household and behaves

And if I lie or sit on the floor he's alongside me within a nanosecond cuddling in.

impeccably in others' homes. We've no shortage of people who say he's a delight to look after and he mixes happily with their dogs. When I go to pick him up, even before I get there he runs around excitedly with a dog-smart sixth sense, long before a human could hear either my car or me.

His world has opened up. He's not dependent on only my husband and me for his happiness which is lovely for him. He'll even let the lady who looks after him most often collect him from his home when we're out. But 'Scruffts' I'm afraid is a no goer as he would baulk if a judge approached him. To all intents and purposes he gives the impression of wanting to interact but the moment a stranger so much as puts a hand out to him in an unknown environment he ducks his head down and swivels away. And I suspect this will always be the case. Occasionally, if someone is particularly keen to interact with him, if I start stroking him he will let a stranger join in but he's got his own selection process for this, the criterion of which isn't obvious.

He will walk for miles but is clearly a senior dog and needs his rest and recuperation. He enjoys a game of football and is a cunning dribbler. Early on he worked out that if he hesitated over the ball it would be kicked for him again. His idea of indoor entertainment is popping bubble wrap and chucking soft toys around, his favourite being a giraffe, with Lion having long since been ragged to pieces.

He likes to play with humans but won't let everyone walk him from our house. And whilst friendly with other dogs and always keen to greet, he nevertheless sees them primarily as an information tool. He marks excessively whilst out on a walk and is intent on gathering information about what dog has been where and when – presumably a throw-back to his street days when survival was dependent on an intelligent understanding of the neighbourhood.

In his second year with us he won second prize for best veteran in a large regional agricultural show. The judge was prepared to overlook his unwillingness to be 'interviewed'. This was close on the heels of coping with a second Monica fundraising gala when he took the noise that had spooked him the year before completely in his stride and came second in the most handsome category.

People have asked me how such a dog could have been overlooked all its life. But it's easy to be overlooked as a human with everything going for you. Even easier as a stray in a country overrun with canines.

Ursu demonstrates emotional intelligence daily. After recent knee replacement surgery, and returning home on sticks, he interpreted this as a game and crouched down in the play position, tail wagging. So I showed him my bloody scar. He smelt it and instantly altered his behaviour, waiting for me to return to him and sticking by me but not attempting to burrow into me in any way until his nose, or my inadvertent behaviour, told him my knee was OK again. In the months before surgery if I was struggling on the downward path and said 'steady' to him he would slow, constantly checking me as to my progress. And speeding up if he judged I was starting to milk it.

Despite his love of balls he never picks up my Pilates circus equipment in the lounge although he likes to join in with my physio programme and so I have decided to capitalise on his body weight and use it to my advantage to let his 17 kilos lengthen tight muscles and ligaments.

As a happy dancer of sorts, years ago my husband treated me to a course of synchronised dancing classes with our then pet, Daisy the retriever. Daisy was already about nine by then and not one disposed to thinking things through too much. As two old bitches together we didn't advance greatly, with Daisy preferring to loll around on the floor rather than do gymnastics through my legs. Had Ursu and I joined forces in some other life I think he would have excelled but it's enough that's he's carefree and happy and we've no inclination to set him bigger tasks. After his cell-ridden bleak life his love of a walk and being outdoors will always be stimulation enough, we think. We've asked him to learn and abide by the rules of socialisation and beyond that he's a free agent.

Just recently Ursu has caught on to picking up a stick in his mouth and carrying it home just for the fun of it. And possibly the biggest shock – he will actually bury a chew in the garden, willing for the first time to consider himself sufficiently well-fed to be able to mentally bypass the opportunity of a treat now for the chance to recover it in the future during possibly leaner times.

He can't tolerate rich food, no matter how nutritious, and his teeth aren't great, what he's got left of them, and he's also beginning with cataracts. Cataracts brought on with age develop slowly in dogs and don't cause them too many problems, particularly with smell being their strongest and most useful sense. He favours his back legs, his back and hips possibly hurt by the dog catchers, or maybe it's just a sign of ageing, but nothing holds him back and the vet agrees we should 'let sleeping dogs lie' unless or until he starts to struggle.

He'll only trust opening a door with his head if it's already a fair way ajar. He's quiet. If he gets stuck behind a door he'll silently stand there – sometimes for up to an hour - until the door is opened for him. If we inadvertently leave food wrappings in our office bin overnight we can be assured the full contents of the bin will be strewn across the floor the following morning.

Of all the wildlife he comes into contact with his fascination is with sheep. He perks up and looks at them intently as if racking his brain to release some long forgotten memory that connects him to them. Another pointer that he probably has some Carpathian Shepherd in him. We trust he's not missing the presence of bears.

A recent delivery note put through our door whilst we were out carried the P.S. 'your dog is super cute.' Ursu had misted up the office glass in his excited barking and wagging of tail wanting the visitor to greet him. So very different from his barking tone when we are in the house with him. It's becoming evident that he's simply alerting us to the visitor. If he's in the garden when someone approaches he'll bark and keep looking back at the house inviting one of us to take over from him. We are his leaders and he's happy with the situation.

What I've learnt

And it's not just Ursu who's been trained. I've always been a lover of animals and particularly dogs, feeling that as humans we share the planet, we don't own it. How Ursu was treated appals me yet there's no glory in having helped save one dog. Animals everywhere are being mistreated by humans, and not just for sustenance, and I am amongst those naively guilty for some of the unnecessary pain. Ursu's ingrained fear has made me re-examine my relationship with animals and made me more conscious of how as a human I harm them.

Early on in my Internet search I read that whilst a dog may be smart it isn't as bright as a human and can be outwitted. I kept reminding myself of this as Ursu and I mentally circled one another, battling to have the last word. He's taught me greater patience and to think more clearly. There is a reason for everything he does and it's my responsibility to understand the motive. Upliftingly, in the same way we can instinctively like and trust another human whose language we don't share, a feral dog and human have been able to bond and communicate through actions and body language. People sometimes underestimate the intelligence of other species and, worse, their right to be treated as humanely as possible, at least by the rich First World countries.

Every day is the same to a dog and it's beholden on me to remain consistent, regardless of whether it's party time for the human. Our only exception to this is during bonfire celebrations when Ursu follows me all over the house seeking protection. A couple of days of consistent calm after the noise abatement and Ursu slots back into the usual routine. Quite rightly my husband pulls me up if I start relaxing into assuming Ursu has human responses, mistakes I made with our previous two dogs, and which I still fall into from time to time. Ursu is obedient and exceptionally content, but doesn't act completely by rote. He understands and welcomes routine and I must continue to be his leader and treat him as a dog and not as a mind-reader.

On a recent trip to Sri Lanka, sat at a table by the beach on the first day, I felt a pressure on my thigh. Glancing down, a male stray had gently placed his head on my lap. There was no food around. It was seeking affection, and maybe a home. I instinctively stroked it before being pulled up by those around me being reminded about the incidence of rabies and my promise to not get involved with every dog I come across. There were strays every few yards, tolerated, if not cared for, by the local people. Dogs, cats and other wild animals the world over needing a life a little better, with humans with the resources to help holding the key to making it happen.

What next? Who knows?

Ursu doesn't do fancy tricks or anything hilarious to post online. He's not saved my life or some other headline grabbing activity. He won't give a paw except on his terms when seeking affection. He still loves his food, and the treat of all raw vegetables, even lettuce, still sets him off prancing and dancing in gleeful anticipation, but he still never asks for his meal. He continues to eat grass, and discarded serviettes also remain a firm favourite, but soil has dropped off his 'must have' menu list.

After two and a half years with us Ursu's natural traits are showing through strongly. He's bright, gentle, inquisitive, playful, affectionate and loyal. And he can be a bit of a rascal.

He likes the people allowed into our home and seeks their affection but ducks away from strangers outdoors. He still barks at the postman if we're not there to command his silence, unless he passes him on a walk when he then couldn't give a fig.

We never thought he would master recall but is very good, and will even sit quietly next to us off lead if we're chatting to fellow walkers. Yet we remain vigilant because such is his navigational confidence, once in a blue moon he'll decide to do his own thing in a kind of 'see you back at base' way. This dog has a mind of his own.

Each time we pick him up from friends after a few days away the bond has grown deeper and he becomes increasingly biddable. It's as if returning to us reinforces his belief that he belongs with us and isn't just passing through. Though, as a typical dog, just when he's been at his obedient best for a sustained period of time he can be guaranteed to commit some misdemeanour.

We've managed to socialize him without losing our patience with him and we've never told him off for an historical offence. Dogs look guilty to appease their evidently cross owner and not because they have any comprehension of what it was they shouldn't have done x hours ago.

It's hard to believe that Ursu has lived with us for about a quarter of the life he led on his own, wild, terrified and unwanted.

What I do know is we love Ursu and it's clear he recognises he's been a lucky dog after years of surviving a pure hell on earth characterised by malnourishment, neglect and abuse. As I write his story he spends much of the time squeezed under my desk eschewing more comfy places to settle. If I'm out of sight and he hears a sudden noise he will come and check that I'm OK, even if it means breaking the boundary rules and risking admonishment.

On the day we picked him up near the M1 one of the female volunteers conversant with his plight said we'd have a friend for life in Ursu, which was difficult to grasp at the time what with all the screaming and bucking and biting. She's been proven right. He's happy, exuberant and adorable and however many years more we have with him will be a blessing. I wish with all my heart that I am with him as he takes his last breath.

I said to my husband when I was desperate to get him out of his Romanian hell-hole that if he did nothing more than sit in our garden on a long lead it would be a heavenly existence by contrast. In reality he has exceeded all expectations and more. Intuitively he recognised the chance being offered him and grabbed it. His hardwiring is still there but his willingness to let go of his past and start over again and begin his trust in humans has been his salvation and I for one salute him. Humans could learn a lot from a dog.

The things we do for dogs.

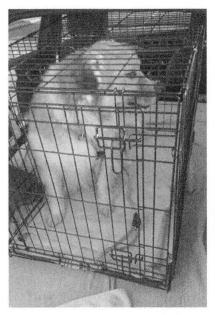

Collecting Ursu on a slip lead.

Early days, still scared.

Enjoying his celery.

Starting to settle in.

Happy days together.   *Just chilling.*

Getting to know the local wildlife!

Waiting for the yes word.

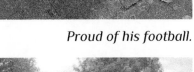

Proud of his football.

Boating holiday.

A winner!

Never give up on a dog

Printed in Great Britain
by Amazon

Printed in Great Britain
by Amazon

36598921R00075